Reverend Bill Crews AM is a much-loved Australian. He has given over three million meals to the poor and homeless. He has also taught thousands of underprivileged kids to read so they can break free of the poverty cycle. His work has been recognised by organisations as varied as the Rotary Foundation and Ernst & Young. In addition, Reverend Crews has been included in the National Trust's list of 100 National Living Treasures and he has been named as one of Australia's 100 most influential people. He also hosts a weekly radio show that is broadcast across Australia.

Twelve
Rules *for*
Living a Better Life

Twelve Rules *for*

Living a Better Life

Reverend Bill Crews
with ROGER JOYCE

HarperCollins*Publishers*

HarperCollins_Publishers_

Australia • Brazil • Canada • France • Germany • Holland • Hungary
India • Italy • Japan • Mexico • New Zealand • Poland • Spain • Sweden
Switzerland • United Kingdom • United States of America

First published in Australia in 2021
by HarperCollins_Publishers_ Australia Pty Limited
Level 13, 201 Elizabeth Street, Sydney NSW 2000
ABN 36 009 913 517
harpercollins.com.au

A catalogue record for this book is available from the National Library of Australia.

ISBN 978 1 4607 5927 1 (paperback)
ISBN 978 1 4607 1297 9 (ebook)

Cover design by Christine Armstrong, HarperCollins Design Studio
Cover photo by Damian Sanchez
All photographs from Bill Crews's collection, unless otherwise stated.
Typeset in Sabon LT Std by Kirby Jones
Printed and bound in Australia by McPherson's Printing Group
The papers used by HarperCollins in the manufacture of this book are a natural, recyclable
product made from wood grown in sustainable plantation forests. The fibre source and
manufacturing processes meet recognised international environmental standards, and carry
certification.

Dedicated to

His Holiness the Dalai Lama,
Dr Bob Wotton, my psychotherapist for over twenty years,
Jon Graham, who helps me find the words to tell my story,
John Singleton, who I love dearly,
and Reverend Shirley Maddox, from whom I experienced
God's loving compassion.

I'd like to thank all the people in my life who have helped me,
especially those I've argued with as they've made my life better.

CONTENTS

FOREWORD
BY HIS HOLINESS
THE DALAI LAMA

I have known Rev. Bill Crews for many years and count him as a friend. On one occasion, at a public talk in Sydney, he introduced me to the audience, half-jokingly, as a good Christian. In my talk, as a result of my genuine admiration for the way he has put loving kindness and service to others in action, especially with regard to the disadvantaged and the homeless, I referred to him in turn as a good Buddhist.

Some of us believe in the power of a loving creator God, others believe in the impact and consequences of our own actions. Be that as it may, the essence of all major religions is the importance of responding to our fellow human beings with love and compassion.

I am happy to say that I had the honour several years ago of visiting Bill Crews at the Ashfield Uniting Church and his

Exodus Foundation in Sydney and sharing lunch with the homeless and volunteers who served them.

In this book – *Twelve Rules for Living a Better Life* – Bill Crews recalls the experiences of his life's journey, both the highs and the lows. I am sure readers will find it enjoyable, instructive and uplifting.

AUTHOR'S NOTE

I am a minister of religion and I constantly surprise myself by how seriously I take that role. To me, being a minister means I look after all those people I come across who need my support. That includes congregation members, staff, volunteers and donors to projects that I run. I see myself as having a 'congregation without boundaries', whether geographical or personal. Everyone should feel they are part of a caring family.

Because my early years were difficult I know what it is like to be 'on the outside', and I feel I have a natural affinity with people who are struggling. I have spent years of my life organising help for them, often without much assistance and more often than not with a great deal of hindrance from Church authorities, local powers, international institutions and governments.

I now believe that my personal involvement with people in need gives me the authority to speak out on issues where people are suffering. It's taken me a long time to write about my experiences and philosophy, but I believe I have something worthwhile to say and the experience and skills with which to say it. And live with it.

Time is running out for me to say and do these things.

On the other hand, I think I'm just getting started.

Something I really want to speak about and share in this book is what I like to call 'The Rules' or 'Bill's Guide to Eventually Living a Good Life'. You'll find twelve rules in the book, each following a chapter about a different part of my life. So Rule #1 follows Chapter 1 and so on.

When I wrote the Rules, I was thinking both of myself and of other people. I know how and why the Rules apply to me, and all the ways in which I fall short of following them, and through this book I invite you to consider how you might apply them in your own life. It's *your* story that is important to you. What's equally important, though, as you read this story of mine, is that you DO as well as REFLECT. The planet is chock-a-block with people who are quite happy to reflect and navel-gaze until the cows come home, but it is the actual *doing* that brings change.

I am the Reverend Bill Crews and, as you can see, I do, indeed, have something to say.

WELCOME TO THE JUNGLE

It was the second most important moment of my seventy-plus years on this planet and it came after more than half a century of helping others.

In 2015 I was suffering through one of the really low spots in my life. For several years I'd been going to London to set up a film festival called the Big Picture, which would showcase films dedicated to social justice. Films that would make you want to go out and do something, films that would get people off their bums and into action, social justice films that would inspire people to change the world. I wanted to bring people into the fold, get them committed to the cause.

The same festival had been really successful here in Australia and I thought maybe I could make it work in England too. I told myself that I'd wanted to do things in the UK for some time, but in hindsight I was probably trying to escape my troubles by temporarily shifting continents. Ironically, I'd gravitated to the place where my father, with whom I'd endured a troubled relationship, had grown up poverty-stricken and fatherless himself. What's more, I was in discussion with the Odeon Cinema Group and its flagship Leicester Square theatre, where Dad had worked as chief projectionist before World War II. Maybe that was another reason I'd been drawn to England.

I had a day free before my flight home to Australia. The news was full of the refugee crisis sweeping across Europe and I wanted to witness it for myself. People suggested I go to Germany and other locations, but I didn't have the time for that. I decided to head to where the most pain was, to 'the Jungle', an infamous refugee camp in Calais, northern France.

The *Camp de la Lande* (aka the Jungle) was little more than a shanty town built by migrants and refugees trying to get to England. At its peak it held 9000 inhabitants. It was officially dismantled by French authorities in 2016, but when I visited, it was bursting at the seams and at the height of its notoriety.

I didn't have a clue what I was doing really, maybe just ticking a box in my depressed state of mind. Go to Victoria Station, get on the train, go to Dover, catch the ferry; just go there. It was only when I stepped off the ferry at Calais that I realised I'd been in such a hurry that I'd left everything behind except my passport and thirty euros. I saw all these taxis lined up, went over to one of them and asked the driver if he'd drive me to the Jungle. No, no, no! It was the last thing in the world he wanted to do. He reluctantly agreed to drive me halfway, but absolutely no further. I asked how much it would cost and he said fifteen euros. I gave him all thirty and told him to come and pick me up at the same spot later. He agreed, and was as good as his word. I've often found that trusting other humans, no matter how unlikely they might seem, pays off.

From the point where the driver dropped me off, I could see masses of people walking on the sides of the road ahead of me, and I simply followed them – the hundreds upon hundreds of refugees looking for any sort of a home. The closer we got to the camp, which was around twenty minutes' walk away, the more people I encountered. Some walking towards the camp and others walking away. All these people walking. Nomads. The lost and the unhappy rejects of the earth.

I now realise that I wasn't heading to the camp just to observe what was going on; no, I was looking for a hell of the earth, because that's where I fit in. Ted Noffs, minister and founder of the Wayside Chapel in Sydney's Kings Cross, used to say that it's in the hells of the earth that you find renewal – and let me tell you, as I walked into the Jungle I was in desperate need of renewal.

It was summer, hot and dusty. The Jungle – haphazardly built over an old chemical waste dump and flood plain – reminded me of some of the Aboriginal camps I've seen in Australia. People were sleeping in a ragtag collection of makeshift tents: under plastic flapping in the breeze; beneath tin, wood and cardboard lean-tos; even under umbrellas. In winter it would have been a sodden, cold, polluted, muddy nightmare. Thousands of desperate people were crammed together in the most appalling conditions, hoping to eventually get to a place of safety.

I've learned, at places like the Jungle, to sit and watch and learn, so that's what I did, observing the mess that was the lives of the inhabitants. There was a heart-rending sign I took a picture of which said, 'When I die, bury me in Palestine and write on my grave I am not a refugee any more.' There were lots of Palestinian flags, lots of displaced Palestinians. There were Afghanis and Iranians, Kurds and Syrians. Sudanese, Somalis, Eritreans. Then I saw a woman who looked like she knew what she was doing, so I approached her. It was Clare Moseley, from Leeds, not long there herself. She'd literally left her business, husband and family back in Yorkshire and travelled to Calais to see what she could do to help. We wandered around together for a while. She introduced me to many residents – all ordinary people in an extraordinary situation, just trying to get by.

Clare was really trying to get things going. She wanted to take action: not wait, but *do*. Soon after we met she quickly and efficiently set up her charity, Care4Calais, to deliver direct aid to refugees sleeping rough in France and Belgium, providing clothes, food and sleeping bags. She now also tries to combat the French and UK governments' policies of refugee deterrence, she campaigns for more tolerance and welcoming of displaced people, and she has started a program in the UK to work with newly arrived refugees.

I saw representatives of many other humanitarian agencies in the Jungle, all quick to announce what they were going to do, but not actually doing it. They were all talk, not like Clare. I've tried to get a meaningful role within one of the United Nations' refugee organisations, but it's really hard, they're closed shops. I've always wanted to get into this area, and I've even got on to David Miliband, the CEO of the International Rescue Committee, a former British Labour Party politician – but to no avail. He's up on the sixtieth floor of a head office in New York, talking about it, but I don't think he often sees what's actually going on, hundreds of metres below him and a continent away in the mud and squalor of places like Calais.

There was definitely plenty of bad stuff going on in the camp: there was drug dealing, there were mini mafias of various ethnicities and they were often fighting. Some groups wouldn't have anything to do with other groups; it was messy.

The second time I went to Calais it was winter and it was snowing. I wandered off on my own and noticed a sign: 'NA (Narcotics Anonymous) meeting at 1pm'. Though not an addict myself, through my experiences helping the drug-affected community in Sydney I know the hope and compassion that can be found in such groups and decided to attend. But where in that godforsaken hellhole could a meeting possibly be held?

I walked down one rutted mud track, searching for another NA sign, then another and another. I asked people and they didn't know. I finally found the meeting after it had started in an excuse for a tent, and was welcomed with a hug. Under a snow-covered tarpaulin, on a carpet thrown over fetid mud sat probably twenty refugees, men and women: Iraqis, Iranians, Syrians, Afghanis, Middle Easterners – rejected people from all over the world.

It was obvious that I wasn't one of them, but no one questioned me being there; they just took me in and made room. There was one guy who was running the meeting and as the others took it in turns to tell their stories he translated in their lingua franca of French mixed with Farsi and Arabic. I couldn't understand a word, but I could see the stories writ large on people's faces as they spoke. In the twelve-step movement they talk about this as speaking the 'language of the heart'. It was there for all to see in that tent on each and every face.

Everyone had spoken, there was no one left except me. All of a sudden it was my time to talk. What on earth was I going to say? Suddenly, in this most desolate place on earth, among abandoned, ignored, rejected refugees, everything caught up with me: my broken marriages; my troubled relationships with my children; my difficult relationship with my father; my sense that I was alone in this world, always on the outside, looking in. I was as lost and low as I've ever been in my life.

All I could bring myself to say was: 'I'm Bill, I'm from Australia.'

It's in the hells of the earth that you find heaven. Signs in Camp de la Lande aka the Jungle, Calais, 2015.

CHAPTER ONE

FATHER AND SON

I was born in 1944 in Hertfordshire, England, in a place called Bengeo, just outside Hertford, the eldest child of Cyril William (Bill) and Barbara Crews. My brother, Bob, was born in 1946, also in England, and my sister, Ann, came along ten years later in 1954, here in Australia.

Both of my grandfathers had died before I was born, ultimately because of World War I. My mother's father got what's called disseminated sclerosis, which begins as a tingling in the fingers and ends up rotting your brain: it's a nerve cell thing and he came back from the war with that. He was one of twelve or thirteen from a wealthy pub-owning family; neither he nor any of his brothers had a son, and their only sister drank the family into poverty.

My grandma on my mother's side worshipped the ground my grandfather walked on and used to talk to me about him all the time. She was from Irish labouring stock, so Grandad's family thought she was beneath him. She worked behind the bar at the pub and one day she and my grandfather were working together and he looked at her and said her name and didn't need to say anymore. My grandmother told me that she knew, she just knew. Aren't all human beings searching for that feeling?

My mum grew up knowing her father had a terminal illness, and he died a few days before her wedding. She and my dad were married in black.

My dad had a different background altogether. His father, a clerk with the Port of London Authority, returned from the war a devastated man, and shortly afterwards he suicided, cutting his throat in a local park. My father was six at the time. During the Great Depression, my father, his brother and their mother were in dire straits. Dad and his brother used to walk the streets of Hackney collecting horse manure and selling it. Later in life, Dad would tell me that story and cry.

My grandma on that side was rather cunning, but perhaps she had to be. When she died, my father found out that she'd been receiving two pensions, both from the UK government. She used to tell both her sons, once they were adults and had left home, that the other never helped her financially, so each boy would generously send her a lot of money. My dad was straight up and down, dinky-di, rigidly moral. Yet he let his mum off the hook, and all he would say was that desperate times call for desperate measures.

All I remember of that grandmother was from when I was really tiny. She'd eventually taken up with another man and was running a pub near the 1904 lighthouse on Dungeness Headland in Kent. I was two or three years old and obsessed with the lighthouse, so she called me Lighthouse Billy.

The earliest memory I have of my parents is at the beach there: I remember Mum and Dad walking away from me along the shingle. Some might say it was a foreshadowing of something that would happen nearly twenty years later. But I don't believe life works like that; it's only hindsight that illogically links certain events together in the mind.

I was three when we left England. Dad, who'd been an officer in the Royal Air Force (RAF) during the war, repairing Lancaster bombers, was the advance party and travelled separately to the rest of us: Mum, her mum, my newly born brother, Bob, and me. Dad travelled with his mate John Green on P&O's SS *Stratheden*, sailing down through the Mediterranean and the Suez Canal. We came on a ship called the SS *Arawa*, which plied its trade between Southampton and Auckland with stops along the way.

Dad and John were heading to New Zealand to make their fortune, and we were to meet them there. John came from a wealthy family, while Dad came from nothing. But John was really good at selling and Dad was really good at buying and they were both obsessed with cars, so they made quite a bit of money in England buying vehicles, doing them up and selling them. Quite often they didn't even need to do the cars up. They were a really good team.

They got to Sydney, where the ship was to dock for a couple of days before sailing on to New Zealand. Dad was walking down Darlinghurst Road in Kings Cross when he unexpectedly bumped into a guy called Frank Stoker, an Australian who had gone to England with the Royal Australian Air Force (RAAF) during the war. Dad had worked with Frank at various RAF bases and they'd become close friends. It had been a huge achievement for Dad, a boy from the slums, to be accepted into the RAF. By his own account, he'd spent a lot of time boning up on general knowledge before his interview and impressed the panel when they asked him – out of the blue – to name the capital of some minor European country. He shocked them when he gave the correct answer. As time's gone on I've been able to see that he achieved a great deal in his life.

Anyway Dad – en route to New Zealand to start a new life – bumped into Frank, whom he hadn't seen since the war, and Frank persuaded him and John to stay in Australia. Dad wired Mum on the *Arawa* and told her to get off the ship in Sydney.

The car business that John and my father dreamed of never came to pass. Dad did a whole lot of stuff, but ultimately formed a company called Blue Mountains Poultry, which shipped frozen chickens to England. He was up against fierce competition like Ingham's, which was already well established, and was doing okay, but then something went wrong and he had to fire someone. The disgruntled employee, as payback, opened the doors of all the freezers and the chickens went off overnight, hundreds and hundreds of them, and Dad had no insurance. He lost everything.

From that day on it was desperation times. We were living out the back of St Marys in western Sydney, and though things were tough I was really happy there. I could wander in the bush on my own, I built a cubby house and there were lots of other kids from migrant families to play with.

Some families lived in hessian humpies in the bush, with roofs made of tin and branches. Other families lived in cow sheds. But everybody was equal, and we all just hit it off.

I went to school at St Marys and was doing really well there. We used to march in and out of school to Sousa's marches, played on old 78s. My closest friend, Noel Rorhlach, was German. He was a Lutheran and I knew I was an Anglican, so it was the first time I realised there were different branches of Christianity, and different religions.

One day Noel and I – we must have been about ten – made a raft and sailed along a creek and eventually came to a glen of tea-trees. I remember lying on the grass, looking up at the sky through the trees and thinking, this is heaven. Years later I was to recreate the memory of those trees and that sky in the design of the Life Education centre at the Wayside Chapel, where we aimed to motivate and empower kids so they could make safe choices about drug use and other health challenges. It stuck with me; it was one of those perfect moments.

I loved everything about St Marys and couldn't have been happier, but it wasn't to last. One day Dad came home and told us we were moving. He had got a job with Vestey's, the cattle property owners and food producers, as an engineer at the meatworks at Riverstone. I was eleven years old and I was devastated.

Our new home would be only twenty minutes from St Marys by car these days, but when you're a kid and you're uprooted from your school and friends, it's really hard. At my new school I was the odd one out – often feeling like I didn't belong. It became a well-known feeling for me.

We were in Riverstone for nine unhappy months. Then we were off again, much further this time. And things were to get much, much worse for me.

My St Marys primary school class, 1955. I'm in the back row at the far left, next to the teacher.

Part of the problem was that I felt that Dad and I didn't really get on. We were quite different. Where he was a 'doer', I, as a young person, was a dreamer. I can vividly remember him trying to push me to get a part-time job, but I was too happy reading and didn't feel the need to earn any pocket money. He wanted to 'toughen me up' and was always telling me not to be so sensitive. He seemed always to be saying, don't be *this*, be *that* – or words to that effect.

I felt that Dad was much closer to my brother, Bob, who not only had an after-school job but was a champion rugby league player too. While Bob was winning awards for his sporting prowess, I was reading, thinking and pondering. I would give my stuff away and Dad would be angry with me. He would physically discipline me, and I was afraid of him. All in all, I felt I was a disappointment to him. I grew to dislike him and hated any behaviour in me that reminded me of him.

I could never quite get a look in with my mother either. Dad dominated her and what he said went. I remember feeling sad looking out a window, watching Mum go to work, walking down a long path away from me. With the birth of my sister I felt even more like the outsider in the family.

*

After Riverstone, Dad got shifted to Townsville, Queensland – 2000 kilometres from Sydney – to be a senior engineer at the meatworks there. Initially I went to Townsville Central State School with Bob, and got on well with the kids there, but when it came time for high school, Dad managed to get me into Townsville Grammar, which I hated.

Townsville Grammar was full of unhappy kids. A lot of them were boarders: there were kids from New Guinea, kids from the bush, kids from the far north – all missing their homes and families and primed to take out their frustrations and heartsickness on each other. Everybody had to join the school's army cadet detachment, where institutionalised violence was rife, even encouraged. I was clumsy, so the cadet sergeant would routinely belt me. One day I made the mistake of wearing the wrong trousers for cadets and the whole school was encouraged to laugh at me. I was bullied and picked on by all and sundry, including the prefects, until it got so bad that one day I lashed out and bashed a kid who was bullying me, and that turned it all around. All of a sudden everyone realised I could fight, but the damage had been done and I desperately wanted to leave the school. But my father wouldn't hear of it.

Years later, the school wanted me to go back to speak as an old boy, and I said, I'm not speaking at that school, they treated me really badly, they can get stuffed. Then the school chaplain called me. He told me that the headmaster wanted to meet with me to apologise. I eventually agreed to attend a reunion dinner, and as soon as I got near the place I felt tense.

I met the principal, who apologised to me, which I appreciated, but what really affected me were all the people there who'd given me a hard time at school. At dinner, I was sitting with one of the guys who'd tortured me and between one course and another he said, 'It was horrible there, wasn't it, Bill, that was a horrible time.' I suddenly realised he'd been through a terrible time too. I could have brought up what he did to me, but I didn't. I just saw the hurt in his eyes. All the Rhodes Scholars the school could boast, all the talk about leadership, the school motto – *Bonus Intra Melior Exi*, which means something like 'Come in Good, Go out Better' – hadn't counted for anything when we were there.

Before I left that night, I paused by the school honour board. The only name from my time at Townsville Grammar on the board was my own. (I'd been appointed a member of the Order of Australia in 1999 for my services to the disadvantaged and my work with homeless youth.) I don't know what I felt about my name being on that board. The school had terrorised me and done its best to break me, but perhaps it had also helped set me on the path to helping others left behind or ill treated by society.

My siblings – Ann and Bob – and me in 1959.

The saving grace of Townsville was that I joined the Boy Scouts and, at sixteen, became the youngest senior scout troop leader in Queensland. My troop won competitions all the time and I loved the outdoor activities. It was in a sense a return to the carefree days at St Marys, roaming the bush, appreciating nature – just with a bit more preparation and organisation.

The assistant scoutmaster wrote a letter of recommendation for me saying I had the makings of a really fine scoutmaster. I read that letter a lot, but I couldn't see the potential in me that he was talking about. Even as an adult I've never felt like a proper leader. I believe I've been a really good second-in-command, but perhaps because of my difficulties with my father, it's not in my nature to consider myself a leader. I've never felt 'good enough'.

We used to go on scout camps, which I came to love, but I remember the first time I was really homesick, so much so that my parents were contacted. They turned up, but wouldn't take me home; they just left me there. I remember them driving off, leaving me howling by the side of the road. It'll make a man of you, Dad told me.

Another saving grace of Townsville was Deacon Hohen House of the Anglican Church, who used to talk about religion to us kids at Grammar; he really impressed me with his understanding manner and lack of pomposity. I also remember being impressed by the Charlton Heston film *The*

Ten Commandments, which I watched in the long tin barn of
the Esquire cinema. Something spiritual, religious even, was
stirred in me by Cecil B. DeMille's 1956 blockbuster shot on
the backlots of Hollywood. I remember walking home in the
dark from the Esquire, telling myself maybe I should become
a priest.

*

In 1960, we were on the move again. Dad was promoted to
be the chief engineer of Metropolitan Ice and Cold Stores, a
subsidiary of Vestey's, located in Harris Street, Pyrmont, and
we returned to Sydney. We lived in Campsie, in the south-
west of Sydney.

There was talk of sending me to Trinity Grammar School,
Summer Hill, but I wouldn't go. I wasn't going to any private
school again, ever! I saw them as cesspits of bullying and
bullshit. So I went to Canterbury Boys' High School and I
remember standing in the playground thinking, oh no, I've
got to make friends all over again. But it was paradise.
I didn't know a school could be like that. There were no army
cadets, you could skip sport if you could work out how to do
it, there wasn't rigorous discipline, yet everybody was clever
and had a good time. Former prime minister John Howard
went there too.

I often say that I wouldn't change anything in my life, not even change all that bullying, because I think it made me a better person, but, oh heck, I lost years of confidence in Townsville and came back to Sydney quite a mess.

I wrote something recently that reflects the trauma of those early years: Real change only happens in really excruciatingly painful situations.

So now I'm not afraid to walk into situations that I know are going to be painful, even though I'll do my best to avoid creating them. I know I'll be better for it. And I know that embracing change can be a wonderful thing.

RULE #1

Cultivate lovingness and compassion.

Love is all that matters. Love matters. Things don't. We can try and fill our lives with all sorts of things and rushing here and there, but love is the only thing that matters.

It's exactly as the Apostle Paul says: without love we become a clanging gong. Love cannot create wealth yet is priceless. Love has no agenda, no gender and no outcome other than itself. It has no expectations and is not conditional. It cannot be controlled, manipulated or exploited. Love just is. The absence of it creates darkness, hopelessness and despair.

The absence of love drives us to fill its place, sometimes with dangerous substitutes. The absence of love creates anger, hostility and misery. Attempting to direct love in the wrong direction creates pain and leaves us unfulfilled.

Love comes and goes in its own time. It defies explanation and is blind and deaf to criticism. Love is at the very heart and centre of all creation and its expression is in healing, building and creating. The tangible and measurable outcome of love is compassion. You can't have one without the other.

This means that to us human beings, relationships are all-important – and probably the most important of these are defined by unconditional love.

In a way, the love expressed in fairy tales is real. As the stories say, we have to be brave enough to go out and either get love or embrace it. I realised through hard experience that the fairy story *Sleeping Beauty* is real. We are all asleep until an outside influence involving love wakes us up.

It was a street person who taught me that true love is unconditional love of the other. You don't love someone for what they can give you, you love them warts and all. 'Your sweetheart is awful to you,' I would say to this street person, and he would respond, 'Oh Bill, she had a terrible childhood.'

I realised he truly loved her. He showed me that love is not a transaction, it just is what it is. So many of us expect things from people we love – as they do from us. That is a mistake.

I have also learned that regarding compassion and love, there are those who 'get it' and those who 'judge it'. I particularly discovered this through my Loaves & Fishes Free Restaurant at Ashfield. Every day over a thousand poor, needy, homeless and lonely people get a free meal. Many people come to me full of praise for the work: they 'get it' and want to be involved. It often brings tears to their eyes. However, there are others who don't 'get it'. They 'judge it'.

'There are people here who are ripping you off,' they say. 'They don't need to be here.'

My answer is: 'If there is one person here who really needs it, it is worth it.'

I find that repeated time and time again through many of life's situations. Often people don't 'get it' until their own suffering makes them reach out for compassionate help – something they, in many ways, didn't realise existed.

CHAPTER TWO

HOMEWARD BOUND

I was finding my way in the world and thinking about career choices. My father was an electrical engineer and I thought that I would follow in his footsteps because that's what you tended to do back then: you voted like your parents and you followed the same career paths. I'd done occupational guidance tests at school, but my parents were so worried when they got the results that they withheld them from me: I'd already more or less decided to become an engineer and they thought that reading the report would confuse me.

Eventually I got to see my vocational guidance report. It said I'd be a good astrophysicist, that I would excel in areas like that; there was no mention of social work. I'm not sure what my parents were worried about.

My father told me once that he would have loved to be a doctor, and I said to him, well, why don't you do it? There he was, slugging it out as an engineer in a slaughterhouse, when he had the brains to do so much more. He said he couldn't put Mum through the poverty of him giving up a good job and becoming a student for such a significant number of years. And what if his dream didn't work out? He'd come from the slums and got through the Depression, had managed to climb out of that and get a good job. He wouldn't risk losing that security. With the arrogance or perhaps naivete of youth, I told my father that he should pursue his unfulfilled dream. This was a man whose own father had ended his life in the most horrific circumstances, a man who, since the age of six, had toiled to lift himself out of poverty, had helped his mother, then moved his family across the world hopefully to a better life. I still wish he'd followed his dream, though.

*

I won a Commonwealth scholarship to study engineering at the University of New South Wales and then I got a cadetship with BHP. But I didn't like the punishing environment in Wollongong so I chucked it in. Dad went and saw someone he knew at Amalgamated Wireless Valve Company, a division of Amalgamated Wireless Australasia (AWA), and somehow talked them into letting me transfer my cadetship. So I worked part-time at AWA and studied at night.

Meanwhile Dad's employment prospects brightened. After Campsie he and Mum, Bob and Ann set off for Tenterfield in the New England region of New South Wales. By that time, I was boarding in a house in Burwood, in Sydney's inner west, while the rest of the family went north. No more moving about for me.

Up in Tenterfield Bob bought an MG TC sports car with all the money he'd made from his after-school jobs. He put big copper pipes on the exhaust so it had the throaty sound of a motorbike; it was the great love of his life.

One Saturday morning in January 1965, there was a knock at the door of my Burwood boarding house. It was my Uncle Frank Stoker, who lived nearby. He'd been sent to tell me that Bob had been killed in a car crash. My brother had been coming home from a dance on a really narrow road, and two drunks were having a race. Bob's car was caught in the middle and he died at the scene of the accident.

Frank had to get home, and I was left alone with my shock and grief.

I wandered the streets of the inner west that afternoon, and ended up at a minister's residence out the back of a church. I couldn't think what else to do or who I could talk to.

I was absolutely shattered, my whole world had disintegrated with one knock on the door, and I was a long way from my family in those days before easy long-distance communication. The minister took me into his office and I told him what had happened. Then he looked at me and said, if you're feeling like that I feel so sad for your poor mother because she must be feeling even worse. There was no compassion for me in his words. My immediate and all-encompassing devastation was replaced by an overwhelming anger. He was absolutely no help at all: he made me feel worse.

He couldn't deal with my emotion. He put a wall up. I was looking for a hug, a kindly word, a shoulder. He ran the other way. My encounter with that minister haunts me to this day.

At some sub-atomic, sub-conscious level, something shifted in me that evening. Amid my untrammelled grief, part of me decided that I would never let an experience like this happen to anyone, anywhere, if I could help it. I've got no sympathy for somebody who sets themselves up to help people and then doesn't.

Yet in a very brutal way that minister, on that night, mentored me. In an ironic twist, he channelled my father and the way he'd often tell me, 'Don't be *this*, be *that*.' From that point on, even though I wasn't able to put it to use for a few years, I made the decision not to be like *that*, but to be something very different, possibly the THIS that I am today.

In the weeks and months that followed Bob's death I remember feeling and thinking that it ought to have been me who was killed, not him, because then my father would not have been so upset. My brother was the apple of my father's eye. He could do no wrong. Bob's death seemed to further distance me from my family; in fact if someone had told me I was adopted I would have answered, 'Why did you take so long to tell me?' I'd grown up jealous of my brother and his easy loving relationship with our father. In some sort of strange way I felt responsible for what had happened to Bob and that spilled out into every aspect of my life; I began to believe that I was the cause of any bad things that happened to people within my ambit. I was more of an outsider than ever.

*

The family moved back to Sydney, so I moved back in with them. I was still working at AWA during the day and going to the University of New South Wales at night. My father used to pick me up after lectures because he knew how hard my course was and how much work I was putting in. At the time I probably took this as my due, never thinking that after a long hard day at work himself, he might have looked forward to a restful night at home.

That vocational report that my parents had withheld from me noted that I had a space–form deficiency, which suggested I had difficulty seeing things intellectually in three dimensions. In practice, this meant it was really hard for me to understand electronic circuits. Without any intuitive understanding, I had to learn them by heart and only with hard work was I able to pass all my subjects. In a way, though, working with solid crystals was a bit like astrophysics, so the 'good' prophecy of the vocational report also kind of worked out in the end.

As a research engineer at AWA I worked with the properties of ultra-pure single crystal silicon to create what are today called integrated circuits. I helped build the first touch telephones, heart pacemakers and computers. Helping in the manufacture of silicon transistor radios was also a big part of my job.

I was doing well; I was successful at work and achieving good marks at uni, but I wasn't happy. I didn't really fit the engineering stereotype: solid, reliable, not thinking outside the box. Even if engineers might be creative in their work, I didn't think of them as creative in living. I had no social life to speak of and working and studying meant long, hard hours. It's not that my future didn't look bright; it did. But in some part of me I knew I was just following the path of my father, not finding my own way.

I felt there must be something more and I spent a lot of my time trying to work out what that 'something more' to life was. As part of this searching I spent my Sunday afternoons at Speakers' Corner in the Sydney Domain, similar to the original Speakers' Corner in Hyde Park, London. Anyone with an issue could stand on a soap box and address the assembled crowd. One of the speakers I was most drawn to was a man of Irish descent called Webster.

John Webster, aka Mohammed Jon Webster, was born in London in 1913 to a father who battled alcoholism and a mother who was in the Salvation Army. His parents were dirt-poor and had twelve children, all of them absolutely brilliant. Webster was a humanist, but along the way had been a fascist, a communist, a member of the IRA and a mystic Muslim. At the time I didn't know any of this, all I knew was Webster. He would be up on his soap box (a ladder in his case) entertaining his audience with his quick, sharp wit. Webster later told me he'd cultivated this out of necessity. His father used to belt him and his siblings and Webster learned he could belt back with words: he learned the sharpness of language that could draw and hold a crowd.

Webster was amazing. He had a real depth of knowledge. He'd recognised early that education was the secret to advancing in life. He used to sit in the London Library and just read books. He worked as a runner for Ramsay MacDonald,

Webster addressing the crowd at Speakers' Corner in the Domain, Sydney, 1974. (© David Barnes)

the first Labour prime minister of Britain. He then dabbled a bit with Oswald Mosley, leader of the British Union of Fascists, and the Brown Shirts. He got caught up with the Salvation Army; he knew Bramwell Booth, who was the son of William Booth, the first general of the Salvos. During the war Webster was interned as an IRA sympathiser and later came to Australia, ending up in Perth in the 1950s. An Ahmadiyya Muslim group looked after him, so he converted to Islam and became an advisor to Gamal Abdel Nasser, the second president of Egypt. Webster knew them all, it was amazing! He reminded me of people like Plato and Aristotle: thinkers and provocateurs who could mouth off and not help but attract a crowd, so magnetic were they. On top of all this, he was gay years before homosexual law reform and nearly a decade before the first Mardi Gras march. He had a spirituality which was uniquely his. He would call out Ted Noffs, the founder of the Wayside Chapel in Sydney's Kings Cross, about Christianity – and his questions would leave Ted struggling for a response. But the two of them got on and there was huge respect between them.

Webster would create newspapers and sell them for twenty cents, flogging hundreds of them on a Saturday. He'd print them off on a Gestetner, an old-school duplicating machine. They were a mixture of madness and brilliant sanity. He would say communism is filth, but Nazism is filthier. He'd yell out, 'Name a Pope and I'll tell you the scandal; name any one of them and I'll tell you the immoral act.' He predicted that the Shah of Iran, with all his millions and all his armies, would be overrun by one man, the Ayatollah Khomeini. He talked about the power of revolutions, and he'd seen many of them.

One Sunday at Speakers' Corner he said he'd be speaking that night at the Wayside Chapel and I thought, I'll go. It was 1970. So I wandered along to a scene I'll never forget. There were all these hippies there and I was a virginal engineer. I was twenty-six and most of the hippies were younger than me. This woman came up to me – Eleanor, we became friends afterwards – and she grabbed me by the testicles. I was like, what, what, what's this?!

I was a single-crystal silicon engineer with a nine to five job, living with his parents in suburban Penshurst. I'd been up and down the country, having landed here from the other side of the world where I was born: how could it be that only there at the Wayside did it feel like I was home? Thanks to Webster, I was taking the first steps on the path to finding my own way.

RULE #2

Trust in a higher power. Just trust.

People think it must be easy for me to believe in God because I'm an ordained minister. It's not! But in my experience it's trusting that leads to faith. Trust doesn't mean you don't doubt, it means you keep moving forward. I have found that if you take a step towards the universe in times of strife, it will take a step towards you. You have to trust – but trust can only come through experience. Faith isn't something you learn intellectually. It comes from learning through experience.

So many of the addicted, abused people I've come across who I thought would be all right have since died, and so many people I've seen who I thought would never be all right have got their act together. You never know what will happen. You simply have to trust and keep moving forward. You will only find faith if you move towards it with an open, accepting heart and mind.

I saw how the absence of trust tortured my father. When Bob died, all the photos of him were taken off the walls. My brother's name wasn't mentioned for thirty years. I don't know how Mum coped when Dad just wouldn't talk about him. Dad was never reconciled to Bob's death and nothing would make him open up about it and talk about Bob. That's the opposite of trust and the opposite of trust is death of the heart and spirit.

Rather than letting go and trusting, people hang on to whatever it is that's killing them or hurting them. Is it because they think they'll crumble if they don't hold on to whatever's propping them up? The reality is they'll get stronger. But how do you help someone across that bridge when they're clinging on to surrender?

There was a woman who came to my church in Ashfield one Christmas Eve. Three or four months before, her son had walked into an oncoming train. She said, I can't face Christmas without him, I've got to come and do something on Christmas Day. She feared that she couldn't live without him. There was another woman there whose daughter had died the year before and, in a way, her story was like my dad's with Bob: the daughter who'd died was the apple of her eye. I found out later the daughter had written a bucket list and one of the things she had written on it was to have Christmas lunch with a homeless person. So the mother coped by helping feed the homeless at our Christmas Day lunch. She brought her husband and younger daughter with her. That woman was obviously the source of strength in her family; her husband seemed to feel in second position to her.

The second year she came, her marriage had busted up, and I was worried about her younger daughter, because the mother did nothing but talk about the daughter who'd died. But the mother kept coming, and one year I finally saw her smiling, and she said, I only come here once a year but I think of you all the time and you're in my DNA because I can come here.

Both women continue to come to the lunch every year. And for every one of these stories I can tell you fifteen more.

We *can* help people across the bridge of clinging on, and how we do it is we sit beside them, literally and figuratively; just sit there while they trust and find faith or they don't. We encourage them just by being there for them. That's how I hope I was with those two women who were both predeceased by a child – a horrible thing. They put their trust in moving forward, step by step; trusted that if they did that they would eventually return to life.

I see lots of kids fighting battles that aren't theirs because they haven't been trusted to be themselves, to find their path – a feeling I can appreciate. Their neuroses are their parents' neuroses. I see it in a lot of leaders whose fathers or mothers assumed and expected, perhaps even demanded, they become leaders, in politics, business, whatever – and that's a form of abuse. Their parents had fixed ideas about them and I see the agony that's caused. I don't think these leaders even know what they believe themselves. The parents wouldn't trust their kids, and the kids can't trust themselves to move forward.

Believe me when I say that my own trust has been really challenged.

On Christmas Day 1964, I drove up the New England Highway to Tenterfield. Bob and Dad met me at the corner of the street. Bob had his MG; he was glowing with pride. I remember we all drove off and a week later Bob was gone. His dog started to howl for him at night and when I got up there I'd try to quieten him, and walk him to this little pond in Tenterfield. One of the neighbours poisoned the dog, gave him meat with glass in it; that was a really dark night. I was a different person then and didn't have the faith that I have now. Maybe it was momentum that got me through, and supporting my parents.

I've had many religious or spiritual experiences in my life since then, often moving me forward when I've found myself stuck. Sometimes I push it; I take a step into the wilderness to see what happens. I take a step into being uncomfortable, I practise trusting. However, I'm not perfect, I'm human, and trust doesn't always come naturally. People say all these things to me – Oh, we love you, Bill, and so on – but I sometimes wonder if I'm liked for me or what someone might need from me.

There's more trusting to be done, I think. And not just by me.

CHAPTER THREE

THE VOICE

In the early 1970s, the Wayside Chapel, situated in Sydney's Kings Cross and pastored by the Reverend Ted Noffs, was the epicentre of the counter-culture movement. Sydney at that time had the largest hippy colony outside San Francisco and practically all of those hippies, along with Sydney's poorest and neediest, spent a good deal of their time at the Wayside.

Kings Cross, aka 'the Cross', is a hop, skip and a jump away from Sydney's centre. Originally famed for its music halls and theatres, following the influx of troops on R&R leave during World War II it became the city's red-light district. The gentrification of the Cross and its surrounding precincts of Potts Point and Elizabeth Bay has long been underway but the destitute, the celebrated, the homeless and the happening crowd somehow still mingle and get along in the Cross, not a stone's throw from the famed Coca-Cola neon sign meeting point.

From that first time onwards, I went to the Wayside every night. At the Chapel's Sunday evening services, I'd listen to various people who would talk about the social justice projects they were working on. But the highlight event at the Wayside Chapel was Sunday night's Question Time, when, in the basement theatre, Reverend Ted would open himself up to questions from the congregation. There would be guest speakers like prominent biologist Charles Birch, evangelical minister Billy Graham, the leader of the Children of God, the leader of the Hare Krishnas, Prime Minister Gough Whitlam, and the racehorse owner and radio station owner John Singleton. I remember a group turning up all bloodied because they'd been at an anti-Vietnam War protest and the cops had beaten them up. Anyone could ask a question. It was a free-for-all. The debates between Ted, Webster and the visiting speakers were something to behold. Maybe because I felt so much in chains at that time, they started me thinking about the idea of freedom.

Indicative of the spirituality and 'religion' that was practised at the Wayside was the Chapel's hymn book *Travelling to Freedom*. It wasn't a hymn book in the traditional sense; it was more of a song book. Compiled by Tony Newman and Peter Stone and published in 1971, it

The Wayside Chapel café (above) and Sunday night's Question
Time in the basement theatre (below). (© David Barnes)

was a hymn book of the times. The readings and songs were unlike any others in a hymn book I'd come across: 'Sounds of Silence' by Simon & Garfunkel, the African-American 'Sinner Man' made famous by Nina Simone, The Beatles' 'Eleanor Rigby', Peter Seeger's 'If I Had a Hammer', and the list went on. It had all the Dylan songs, all the Peter, Paul and Mary songs.

It documented the music and feeling of the day. I still have and treasure my well-thumbed copy, one of the few, I think, in existence. This book was important to me; it was one of those things that changed my life.

I came from a relatively 'normal' middle-class home. It was not really religious at all. The only time I remember us all going to church was when Bob died. I was blown away both by the bohemian atmosphere and the sheer need of the unfortunates approaching the Wayside Chapel for help. 'If you're not part of the solution, you're part of the problem,' said Ted, the charismatic pastor, the showman, dressed all in white – white suit, white shoes, white shirt, white tie – challenging the crowd.

I quickly decided that I did not wish my life to end with me feeling I had been part of the problem, and so volunteered to help. I'd volunteer in the coffee shop and on Saturdays I'd go and visit the old ladies in the neighbourhood who were being literally terrorised by property developers like

Frank Theeman who wanted to tear down the Victorian terrace houses in the area and replace them with soulless, profit-turning high-rises. I was caught up in all of that, and well remember the disappearance a few years later of Juanita Nielsen – an activist and local journalist who spoke out against Theeman's plans and the eviction of dozens of residents from their homes on Victoria Street. It was an ugly time.

Very soon I wasn't just listening to the Sunday service and the ensuing Question Time, I was helping run them, reading psalms, and when Ted started a crisis centre, I became part of that. It was a drop-in and call-in centre for people in trouble. As it grew, we were face to face with all the traumas experienced by people living in Kings Cross and elsewhere. The drugs, the sex, the American soldiers on R&R from Vietnam. The runaway kids. The corrupt police. And over and over, the drugs.

I was home. They were all my brothers and sisters. The counsellors and the people in trouble were my family. It was magic. We were a group, a tribe, and unlike Townsville Grammar or AWA, this was my tribe.

As a volunteer at the Chapel, the first thing I was asked to do was drive the Chapel jeep somewhere. I'd never driven a four-wheel drive before. But whoever was with me said it's easy, just get in and drive it. I did, I drove it. It was the first time I realised I could do something capable and useful that wasn't part of the path my parents wanted me to walk down. I had all these sides to me that had been blocked or imprisoned. I was full of abilities and competencies and stuff that my father thought wasn't important, but most of my being had been submerged, pushed down. The Chapel showed me that there was more to me than met the eye. Ted Noffs was part of my opening up, and in many ways I looked on him like God. Or perhaps as a father.

Ted wasn't just part of the Wayside Chapel, he *was* the Wayside Chapel. He was charismatic. He was accepting. He was open. He talked religion in a way that I could understand. He was nothing like the minister who'd turned me away when Bob died; he was more like Charlton Heston's Moses, preaching a religion I could relate to with all its pain and foibles, contradictions and mess. Ted was a walking contradiction. His head was in the clouds but he had feet of clay.

One of the most moving times I remember was sitting with him in the coffee shop and a young woman came in who was a mess; she was all over the place, crying, and she said, ah Ted, this happened and then this happened and then he said this and I said this and she did that, on and on and on. Ted looked at her tenderly and said, 'Darling, were you born in August?' I was surprised by the question. But through all her sobs the woman managed to nod yes, and he said, 'So was I, I understand completely.' He listened and connected and then sat with the woman until she was calm.

Ted was the classic Leo in his white suit, white shoes, white everything. He'd been to one of the big theological colleges in America and he'd studied rural theology. On his return to Australia, the Methodist Church hierarchy sent him to Kings Cross, probably one of the most urbanised areas in Australia and hardly steeped in rural theology. But if it was a joke, it backfired. Within a year of his arrival, Theodore Delwin 'Ted' Noffs, Methodist (later Uniting Church) minister, took a single room under a small block of flats in Hughes Street, Kings Cross, and expanded it into a chapel, coffee shop, theatre and community drop-in centre – the Wayside Chapel we know today.

There was a guy there called Gerry Attrill, a clinical psychologist who Ted had put on, and though he was mad as a snake he started what were called encounter groups, based on the philosophy of the Gestalt movement. They included a lot of primal therapy, which really started to liberate me because I was pretty neurotic. My father still dominated my life and I remember one time getting really angry and thumping at a pillow while Gerry yelled, 'Thump it, thump it, thump it!' The depth of anger and frustration and sorrow and need in me was bottomless back then.

By night I would be at the Chapel and by day I'd go back to my job at AWA. There was a production line staffed by women – because in those days male employers thought that all women were good for was repetitive tasks – putting electronic valves together. I made a point of hugging every woman on the line when I arrived at work. I wanted them to know I saw them as people of value and interest; they weren't mere 'economic units'. The women loved it and the men thought I was a bit odd, but because engineers are a bit odd anyway it was more or less accepted, which today it wouldn't be.

Whether it was the combination of working with needy people and participating in the church services and seeing work through new eyes I'm not sure, but within a few weeks my visits to the Wayside Chapel led me to undergo a profound religious experience.

One evening, at the Chapel, I was going up the stairs to the coffee shop to do my shift and I got to the landing. It must have only been a millisecond in which all I'm about to tell you took place. Yet time seemed to stand still. I cannot say that I literally heard a voice, but it was a *knowing* and to this day I've spoken of it as a voice. It just happened as I paused momentarily on the landing. The 'Voice' said to me: 'You are to leave your job and come and work here. You are to work with the poorest of the poor. The work will be hard and unrelenting, but I will be with you. The work will be onerous, but I will help you keep at it. I will guide you. You will become well known but don't worry about that. And by the way your personal life won't be that happy. But I will be with you.'

It was the last bit that made me realise it was real. If it had been all flowers and sunshine and happy music and I was told I would be happy forever and that I'd be rich, I wouldn't have believed it. But because the good stuff, the success, was leavened with the not so good, that's what made me believe, made me trust.

I have found that most people who have these sorts of experiences come from a fundamentalist Christian background and are confirmed in their prejudices and preconceptions by what they hear. My experience was almost the opposite, urging me to change my life completely and opening me up to a wide range of religious and spiritual thoughts and experiences. I embraced the multiplicity of religious and spiritual beliefs of the counter-culture as well as those that were more traditional, be they Buddhist, Hindu, Muslim, Jewish and so on.

Whatever had taken place going up those stairs, it was as if the sun had come out for me. Bang! Just do it.

I went to AWA the very next morning and said, I've got to leave; I have to go and work at the Wayside Chapel. I didn't talk it over with anyone. It was difficult, because AWA had invested a lot of money in me, in my studies. I remember I was crying and upset. 'I just have to go, I have to go,' I said. There was no looking back.

By comparison, telling AWA was the easy part, because then I had to go home and tell my parents. I had to tell my father. It was really hard, but I had no choice. I was turning my back on a promising career, a well-paid job I'd studied for, that others envied, a position Dad had gone out on a limb to get for me.

My father disowned me. It was terrible. He said I needed psychiatric help. I was so affected. I don't have much memory of my mum during this period, I can't remember what her feelings were. I was numb.

For the past fifty plus years I have in my own imperfect way tried to stay true to that Voice. In many ways I feel like the Apostle Paul who uses the word *doulos* to explain his relationship with God. *Doulos* means slave/servant. I know rationally I can walk away from the Church and my ministry at any time, but emotionally I can't. Sometimes I wish to hell I could. I could have ignored or denied the Voice, but I didn't. I could have stayed at AWA, but I didn't. I could have made my father proud, but I didn't. I now know I never could. Towards the end of his life, I could see he was proud of me but it seemed to me, in the mindset I was in then, to be because I was well known.

RULE #3

**A tree will grow in fertile soil. Sandy soil
will stunt it. It is true for human beings too.
We need to find the right company.**

In Kings Cross one day, the local Rotary Club decided to do a fundraiser for the Wayside Chapel. They had an auction, and my job was to collect the stuff to be auctioned. As I was bringing the stuff in, people would say to me, I'll give you a hundred dollars for it now. It was so easy to get bent in that environment. It was a time when some very dark activities were going on, and there were places in the Cross that I wouldn't let any of the other Wayside volunteers go. I knew how corrupting it could be.

I'd wander through the most disreputable sex clubs, looking for young people to rescue. I'd do it often and yet never became corrupted by the squalid environments I found myself in. It would have been so easy to start thinking of that way of living as okay; I saw good people get corrupted by it, caught up in the system and changed.

I was talking to a kid a few years later who had been clean and sober for a long time. Then there was a drama in his life and for about a week he started drinking and using. He said, this guy, a dealer, keeps texting me to sell me stuff and I don't want it anymore. I said, dob him in. He said, oh no, I can't do that.

Years later I took a more active role with Gypsy, a guy who was selling drugs to a lot of the kids I was looking after at Ashfield. One young user, a client of Gypsy, ultimately died. We used to get him clean and Gypsy would sell him dope and he'd be crook again; the merry-go-round kept spinning. I banned Gypsy from Exodus, so he'd sit at the bus stop opposite and he'd sell drugs to the kids from there. I rang the cops and got them to take him away and rough him up. I couldn't do it today. He never came back, but it was the only way to keep the kids safe.

I've got a team with me today who are really good and we can sit and talk with kids in a loving environment. A lot of the church environments I've seen are unhealthy because they're gossipy; I think they're designed to keep people in line in an unhealthy way. If I had a choice between sitting with a group of church people and sitting with a group of twelve-step people like the welcoming open-hearted souls at the Jungle in Calais, I'd choose the twelve-step people, because they're trying to help each other get and stay healthy. That's what I try and do: I try and create a healthy environment so people can grow and make healthy choices, because we can all be tempted.

There was this guy I knew, he was a thug and a crook and he had a son who was born with severe disabilities. This guy, the crook, loved his kid like you wouldn't believe; it just brought out all the good side of him. He decided to run a fundraiser for him and asked me if I could come and speak at it. It was full of all these 'characters' and I'd ask them what they did for a living, and each one would answer a bit of this and a bit of that. They'd got their hands on some Australian football jumpers and they were forging the signatures of various footballers on them, to sell them for more money. They had Kerry Packer's polo gear and got his personal assistant to wear it, and as it was being sold they auctioned her off as well! The crook raised a lot of money.

What am I trying to say? That it was an unhealthy environment and the Cross was an unhealthy environment in general, but there was a lot of love there too and you had to know which was which. And some of the people there were the fertile soil for me and the counsellors, the team I put together around me.

I've grown into the person I am – I've been successful and effective, some might even say loved – so obviously there's been fertile soil along the way. Whatever the mixture of soil in places like the Cross – fertile and toxic – it helped me grow here in Ashfield. There are oases in any wasteland and you have to look for the fertile soil and irrigate and nurture it, so that people can not only survive but thrive and grow.

Like two of the homeless kids I took in at Ashfield: Jese and Lois. They'd sleep in the church. Neither was born in fertile soil. Now Jese works in Western Australia and Lois out Cabramatta way, in south-west Sydney. They're both married and like a brother and sister to each other. What I tried to do with them was create an environment where there were possibilities, to create fertile soil where there had been none. That's what I'm still trying to do.

There obviously have been times, like with Gypsy, when the only way to deal with toxic soil was to get the cops involved. And there have been many times when the only way was to get down in the gutter with the people who were floundering. That's what I learned in the Cross. Sometimes the 'good' methods are just not going to work and you have to either take tough action, or make yourself vulnerable and just try to listen to and reach people.

I'd say the end justifies the means. It can be hard because you put yourself at risk sometimes or you risk demoralising good people trying to help. One of those Ashfield kids, Jamie, sneaked out at night, went to the school across the road and began to graffiti the place. A gang of kids called the Burwood

Bombers used to graffiti that school regularly. They saw our kid on their turf, grabbed him and sprayed him from head to toe with his own black paint. He came home dripping with the stuff, and we had to try and get it off him. We had to cut all his hair off and scrub him with steel wool, and eventually his skin looked deathly pale. It was as if he was terminally ill. About three days later there was a knock on my door and there stood the captain and the deputy captain of the primary school where this had all taken place; they were about eleven or twelve. They said, we've seen the dear little boy you're looking after who's dying of cancer and we've taken up a collection for him and here's the money. I couldn't tell them he was well and healthy and had been trying to vandalise their own school. I just said thank you very much. Why would I ruin their goodness and willingness to help others? Those kids were growing in the right soil and I had no wish to pollute it.

If you look, you see those stories everywhere. They affirm that you're on the right path, maybe in the right soil.

CHAPTER FOUR

THE PASSION OF THE CROSS

I love the Cross, I love it with all my heart and soul.

In the 1960s, when my father worked for Vestey's, he developed the first automatic ice-selling machines. I spent a couple of New Year's Eves in Kings Cross with him, monitoring some newly installed machines, making sure they were working properly. That was my earliest taste of the place that was to become my often unrequited love.

Ten years after those first visits with my father, my knowledge of the Cross grew fast. After resigning from AWA, I approached Ted Noffs and asked him for a job. He was happy to employ me as he knew I was a hard worker and 'got' what he and the Wayside were trying to achieve.

'What's the least amount of money I can pay you?' he asked. Gerry Attrill was starting a commune in Woolloomooloo which cost ten dollars a week and I wanted to be a part of it. 'Eleven dollars a week,' I responded. And so I went from a research engineer's salary to eleven dollars a week.

I lived there for a while. There were about seven of us. Most of the others followed an American spiritual teacher called Baba Free John aka Da Free John. It was the early 1970s and communes were springing up everywhere following the Summer of Love. It was a time of music festivals, peace and transcendental meditation. It was also a time of hallucinogenic drugs, opiate-based drugs, drugs you could smoke, drugs you could inject, drugs you could inhale, drugs you could eat – drugs were everywhere. Even so, we were all on the same path, living in the commune together, all going to the Wayside.

It all started to fall apart when a girl who hung around the Wayside became really ill and had to go to hospital. She had a little boy and I said I'd look after him until she got better. I took him to my parents' place, thinking we could stay there, and they freaked out. I had to take the kid back to the commune. It didn't turn out well. The boy was sick too, it turned out, and we all ended up getting hepatitis. I was really ill and had to go back home to my parents to be looked after. While I was recovering, the commune imploded.

I stayed at home for six months; it was a long, slow recovery. I was really locked into myself, writing lots of poetry when I was well enough to do it. I could see my mother was really angry and didn't quite know what to do. She then got sick with hepatitis too and both of us took years to fully recover.

I was really nervous about going back to the Chapel. With the demise of the commune I didn't know if I would fit in anymore. I'd burned my bridges with AWA and had spent my recovery writing poetry, so I didn't have much to fall back on.

When I finally went back to the Cross I was so low and felt so bad about myself that I couldn't walk into the Chapel. I stood across the road, pretending to look in the shop there and all the while I was looking at the reflection in the shop windows of the people going into the Chapel, trying to work up the nerve to go in myself. There were people coming and going, new people, old people; a lot of the people I knew seemed to have moved on. Eventually I gave up my window shopping and crossed the street.

Ted had fired everyone who'd been in the commune, but of course he was still there and the crowds were still there. You had everybody from the Australian ballet dancer and choreographer Sir Robert Helpmann to strippers, show girls and down-and-outs. There were film stars and politicians –

Ted Noffs in full flight at the Wayside Chapel, 1974.
(© David Barnes)

Gough Whitlam, the twenty-first prime minister of Australia, and his predecessor William McMahon – all the gurus and swamis, captains of industry, everybody. There was nothing like it anywhere. People just dropped in and hung out. Ted had based the running of the Chapel on the Glide Methodist Church in San Francisco, which had been a counter-culture rallying point of the 1960s, but it was really nothing like Glide. It was just a unique coming together of a whole lot of circumstances.

It's fair to say that I clung to Ted Noffs as a sort of father figure while I was getting blowback from my actual father. And it wasn't just my family I was estranged from; I'd also lost almost all the friendships I'd made at AWA. There was one guy called Phil Smith, an engineer, whom I was friendly with – his parents were fairly senior in the Wesley Mission. He understood and kept in touch, but not many did. I was a bit of a loner anyway. As the years went by, quite a few dropped in to say hello, including my old boss Doug Sutherland. I realised they were really proud of me for doing what I did. That was quite a thing to learn.

At the Chapel I had to find new people, new friends. David Barnes became a really good friend of mine: he was the crisis centre photographer, more or less capturing everything. My friend Tim Roberts, who's now a senior producer for CBS New York, Henry Martin, who was one of the ministers, and David Parrot from the 101st US Airborne, who'd been damaged by his time in Vietnam, were part of the crisis centre team. There were many who sought our help, but one I'll never forget is Lillian.

Early on during my time at the Chapel, Lillian overdosed in her unit and we had to keep her awake until the ambulance arrived. With another guy I walked her up and down, up and down, and kept her alive until the ambulance came and saved her life.

Lillian had been a registered nurse's aide in New Zealand and she and I became friends. We used to meet regularly, and because she was dyslexic I wrote out a summary of her life story on two pages of an exercise book and numbered each line, so it was as if her life ran from line one to line sixty. I put her life in order and we'd talk about it line by line so that she could get things together. We did that for years.

Lillian did get her act together and the Lillian Howell project, which provides care and supported housing for girls and young women, is named after her. She became a real character of the Cross, this big, loving person. Everybody knew her. Seven years after I first met her we got news that she'd died. We were all broken.

Ted conducted the funeral and a few days beforehand asked me to speak about Lillian. I was sitting in my office at the Chapel, wondering what I'd say, because there were so many good things to say about Lillian – she was such a good woman – when I picked up a pile of papers and there was the exercise book with her life story in sixty lines. I hadn't seen it for years. I opened it, and at the end of the sixty lines Lillian had added an inscription: 'Bill, you have been so lovely to me, I am writing this to thank you for everything you have done. For the past few years, words cannot say how much I am gladful I met you.' I'd never seen it before. I walked into the funeral and told the story.

In the Cross, at the Wayside, there was story after story after story.

Before my illness and six months away, there'd been a young woman, Barbara, who kept coming to the Chapel, looking at me and saying hello. Barbara was still there when I returned and we started talking, and eventually I moved into her place just around the corner from the Wayside. A while later a group of us hired one of those Halvorsen Cruisers and went on a cruise on the Hawkesbury River. Most of us set off on a walk once we'd moored and when I got back to the boat a bit before the others I found Barbara onboard alone, crying. I asked her what was wrong, and she said she'd been told she had cancer and was dying. That was it, we got married.

Barbara had been a Barnardos kid, one of the many vulnerable children cared for by the organisation founded in Britain in the late nineteenth century. She had been brought over here from England by Barnardos, who'd told her she could ride a horse in Australia, but she had been treated very poorly in her new home on the south coast of New South Wales.

Barbara fell pregnant before our wedding and my father, with whom I was in an uneasy truce, disowned me for the second time. Then, just before we were to be married, I found a wedding photo of Barbara and another man. She'd been married to this guy and they'd had two children down on the south coast. Her husband had been electrocuted and died and the children were living with his parents, who wanted nothing to do with Barbara.

We managed to sort through that, but then had to face something else. Barbara was a twin and her sister, Beryl, the other twin, was also pregnant, but further down the track in her pregnancy. At twenty-four weeks, Barbara started bleeding in the bath and I rushed her to hospital, wondering why this was happening as she'd been happy and healthy to that point. Impulsively, I checked to see whether Beryl had given birth. She had, that very day. I was left with the feeling that some magical connection had caused Barbara's bleeding.

Barbara kept bleeding from the day Beryl gave birth, and the hospital kept pouring blood into her as fast as she was losing it. After five weeks Barbara developed heightened anti-Kell antibodies, which exposed the baby to the risk of severe anaemia. He would have to be induced at only twenty-nine weeks and the doctors didn't know if either he or Barbara would survive.

That was one day when Ted really shone. He came and sat with me and Barbara and we all talked, then he asked me to leave him alone with her for a while. They prayed and then Barbara was wheeled into the operating theatre and next thing I knew they were rushing this tiny little newborn wrapped in aluminium foil to the Prince of Wales Hospital at Randwick. Barbara was in the Royal Hospital for Women in Paddington, our baby son Michael was in Randwick, and the doctors still didn't know if either would survive.

Barbara had a hysterectomy and was soon taken off the critical list. However, Michael was not out of the woods by a long shot. The medical staff told me that if he lived an hour, he'd live two; if he lived two hours, he'd live four; if he lived four hours, he'd live eight. I remember them pumping something into his spine with a huge needle because they said he might have meningitis, and him screaming. I spent my mornings at the Wayside Chapel running the crisis centre and in the afternoon I'd go and see Barbara. At night I'd visit Michael.

Something happened in the midst of this that really affected me. I had left Michael's ward at Prince of Wales late one cold, wet July night to go home and was passing a phone box in the back blocks of the hospital when the woman inside it called to me. I didn't know who she was. She said, will you hold me, because she had to ring her husband in Albury and tell him their baby was dying, was going to die that night, and she couldn't do it without someone holding her. It was like a sad movie set, a solitary phone box in the dark and the rain and the wind, and I held her as she rang her husband and they both sobbed their hearts out and I did as well, because their baby was going to die and I knew my own baby could die at any minute too.

Following that experience at Prince of Wales, I got a team of volunteers to go to the hospital to sit with sick kids. It was way back in the 1970s and there was one case that really unhinged one of the volunteers. There was a little boy dying and the doctors had told his parents not to visit anymore because it was too painful for them. The little boy said to the volunteer, 'My mum and dad don't love me anymore.' What do you say to that? The doctors had acted with good intentions, but it was the child who suffered, and probably the parents later too. How I wish those parents had stepped into their pain, trusted, and kept moving forward, easing the way for their little boy on his last journey.

Michael survived and came home and everything was rosy and happy for a couple of years. We were living in Parkham Street, Surry Hills, and I especially remember a beautiful

August day, one of those perfect days with the bluest of skies and the greenest trees. I remember Michael running in the back yard. The Johnny Nash song 'I Can See Clearly Now' was playing, and Michael picked up a stick, called out, 'Dad', and I looked over to him. He was in the sunlight and I remember thinking, I'm really happy. Michael was healthy and it could have turned out so differently: he could have died, Barbara could have died. We were a happy little family, or so I thought.

Within two weeks Barbara left. She was gone, vanished, leaving her husband and child behind. I had no idea why. I was gutted. Michael was two years and ten months old.

Barbara's life had been difficult: she was an orphan, she'd been abused. She remembered being taken to a place, a school or orphanage in Aylesbury, Buckinghamshire, when she was really tiny, and being put in a bed. She could hear the noise of the kids all around her and thought it was really lovely, she felt part of everything, and then somebody turned the lights out and the kids went silent and she screamed. She screamed for her mum and her mum never came. So I don't think she ever had the skills to be a mum herself.

*

When my marriage to Barbara broke up I was devastated: one day everything was happy and the next day she was gone and I was destroyed. And because of my emerging public profile, the marriage collapse made it into the press. I was sitting on the steps outside Wayside feeling miserable when this street guy I knew called Cliff, an Aboriginal man, came up and said, 'Ah mate, fucking dreadful. I've heard what's happened, I've come to sit with you.'

Cliff was a lover not a fighter. A member of the Stolen Generations. An alcoholic. He'd drink aftershave and he'd often smell of California Poppy hair tonic. He used to come up at night and we'd talk as I was running the crisis centre. One day Cliffy pinched a whole lot of my stuff and I called the police. He went to jail and I worried that would break our friendship, but it didn't. There was something powerful and beautiful about Cliff, sitting there on that step outside the Chapel, trying to make me feel better.

Something similar happened at Ashfield when two of the people who drop in here a lot came by one day and said, 'Bill we've got all this stuff to hock and we need the train fare to go and hock it.' I gave them the money – and then found the stuff they'd pinched was mine. I rang the police and they got prison for it, but they came back a year later and apologised. 'We were so addicted to heroin,' they said, 'we just had to do it and we're sorry.'

Just like Cliff. He'd get so drunk and yet he'd be there for you if he could be.

*

I learned quickly at Wayside how hard it is to maintain integrity. I really wanted to be a source for good there. The crisis centre had a blanket rule of no sex with the clients. Anyone who did had no place in the centre.

We were all people looking for something and the people who came to us for help were really vulnerable and it was easy for volunteers and staff to fall into relationships with them if they were so inclined, and it wasn't healthy. There was a grey area between helpers and helped. There were a lot of sexual predators hanging around, males and females, and I didn't want to be part of that. In all my dealings with people there I was rigidly moral.

I brought up Michael without a partner for a long time. The whole crisis centre team became Michael's parents: we all looked after him, everybody looked after everybody else. Michael was brought up by a community. It helped that we were living right next to the Wayside. I remember Jim Wills, the one-time managing director of St George Bank, doing his bit. And I remember Christine, one of the crisis counsellors, looking after Michael one evening when I was running a meeting. She put him in the bath, then decided she'd get in with him. She said Michael's eyes nearly fell out of his head. It was very communal and I miss that with all my heart, even now.

Time passed, and another person turned up who would take a co-leading role in my life. It was 1976. At first, Gill and I just used to talk a lot. She came from another troubled family background and was trying to get her act together.

Not long after we met, Gill went off to New Zealand and I really missed her. She returned to the Wayside as a follower of Bhagwan Rajneesh, an Indian 'godman' and leader of the controversial religious movement named after him. She also came back with a partner, a guy I knew who had been my sister's boyfriend at school in Penshurst. I'd been holding a candle for Gill with absence fanning the flame, and out of nowhere she was on the arm of another.

They busted up only a few months later. I remember the day well, because I was running a group at Mount Druitt for really wild kids. We used to show classic horror movies and the teenage girls would bring their older boyfriends, and on this particular occasion one of the girls went off with a boy other than the one she was supposed to be with. There was a big fight and one of the boys turned on me and knocked me out cold. I ended up in hospital. I was okay, just bruised, but a couple of days later Michael had a fit at home. Gill and Lillian came out of nowhere and fixed him; they got him to hospital. He'd had a febrile convulsion and I was so glad they were there. Somehow things just happened with Gill after that. Affairs of the heart never travel along a straight line, but

My good friend Tim Roberts with my son Michael and me.
(© David Barnes)

we ended up being together for a long time. A year after the Michael scare we were married.

Gill was one of the many people who came to the Wayside Chapel and I think we were able to cope together because it was such a bohemian place, the atmosphere was conducive to a couple like us. In straight society we probably wouldn't have worked out. Gill eventually became one of the helpers. She got right into my soul.

*

Gill really wanted kids, but nothing happened for a long time and we decided to adopt a baby from India. We'd even named her: Indria. The day we were to sign the final forms, Gill found out she was pregnant and we went through the agony of deciding what to do about the adoption. We decided in the end that we had to say no; it wasn't an easy decision nor one taken lightly, nor something I'll ever forget. Across the years and decades there's always been a hole in Gill's and my heart for a little baby called Indria.

Gill's pregnancy was really touch and go for a long time, and one night she started bleeding. Her doctor swiftly organised a transfusion which saved her life. The birth of our baby, Emelia (Eme), was traumatic too. The umbilical cord was wrapped around her neck. I hadn't known a birth that was easy. But one of the beautiful things I remember was Michael – who was twelve at the time – sitting beside the humidicrib with his fingers through the holes, holding Eme's hand.

Our second daughter, Alexandra (Alex), was born less than two years later. By the time Tim came along to complete our family, Gill's liver was becoming problematic, so it was again a difficult birth. We later discovered that the blood given to Gill prior to Eme's birth had been contaminated. Gill had contracted hepatitis C.

RULE #4

Find a help group to share your growth journey with.

The Wayside Chapel and Kings Cross attracted a unique group of people. There's a unique group of people here at Ashfield too, working at the Rev Bill Crews Foundation or taking part in our programs. Hopefully – years from now, when I'm not here – somebody's going to learn something from me and they'll set up somewhere else. Like me, like Ted. It was the start I got from Ted in the Cross that enabled me to set up at Ashfield. I was with Ted at the Wayside for thirteen years, from 1970 to 1983. It's as if my bones were formed in Kings Cross and the flesh has grown on them in Ashfield.

The Wayside group was my family, my tribe; we thought a lot the same. Coming to Ashfield, I met people with a completely different mindset and culture.

*

Years ago, at the Wayside, we got a fish tank and filled it with fish. Eventually all the fish died and the fish tank was stored away. Then the craze shifted to mice. We bought two mice and treadmills and ladders for them to play on. Unfortunately, they were male and female and so the two mice became eight, and pretty soon there were dozens of them.

At first it was lovely to see all these little mice running around, but then we found a half-eaten one and we realised something not nice was going on. The mice were getting really aggressive and we didn't know what to do, so I sneaked out in the middle of the night with the tank under my arm and let them loose in a dark lane. God help any rats that were in the vicinity!

I began to realise that human beings have an 'event horizon' around them, like the walls of a fish tank. That is, a boundary beyond which nothing seems to make much impact. An event from outside that boundary might get through, but only dimly – as it's events within the boundary that matter. Some people have a large horizon but for others it is very close, and my guess is that is why it is so hard for some people to understand others.

For many the event horizon is limited to events within the family and even within the home. They can't see how politics impacts on their lives and so in many ways are disengaged from wider society. For others, the circle does not extend much beyond their own 'aura' and they can be very selfish in their approach to life. If we try to look beyond our limited horizons to find souls we can find some rapport with, maybe even bond with, we will develop and grow. We need to realise the world doesn't revolve around us, that we're one of ten billion or whatever it is and we'd better start sharing with those in need, whether they be homeless kids right here in Sydney or Muslim refugees yearning for a new life in the ghettoes of Calais.

When we're stuck inside a boundary with people who think and feel exactly as we do, as many social media users seem to be, we implode, just like those trapped mice at the Wayside.

CHAPTER FIVE

I WANNA KNOW WHAT GOD IS

Shortly after I joined the Wayside Chapel team, I became involved with a well-known couple who were trying to have a baby. This was in the early 1970s, when there was no IVF or anything like that. The couple had been trying for years and nothing had happened. They had been to specialist after specialist who could find no reason for them not to become pregnant. I talked with them over many weeks and in the end they decided to adopt. Their desire to have a child was so strong.

Of course, the day they went to sign the adoption papers the woman fell pregnant, as was often the case in those days. As I've already mentioned, the same thing happened to me and Gill. I think it has something to do with the tension falling away.

Their baby was born with great rejoicing. There was happiness everywhere and I felt quite pleased with myself for being with them through this time.

Then one morning I was woken by the phone ringing – it was about 4 am, I think – and the mother was screaming down the phone. Their baby had mysteriously died in a cot death. When she called me, the baby was still in the cot.

After the authorities left, the couple came to talk with me and it was a terrible grief-stricken time. The three of us sat in unbelievable sadness. We just sat and talked and cried and shouted and screamed and hollered. She was very beautiful, with long blonde hair that now hung unkempt and matted. Distraught, she kept shaking her head and running her hands through her hair.

The conversation wafted and waned and at times became very deep. Then I noticed she began talking about her brothers and her sisters, her family, her parents, her husband – in a way, she was listing everyone she loved. And she talked about how much she loved them.

Sitting there, I was struck by the fact that in the very depths of her grief, all she was talking about was love. As she talked, I was looking intensely into her eyes and I reckon

I saw right into her very soul. Right inside I saw a tiny, little candle flame. It was almost out but it was flickering in the darkness.

The words in St John's Gospel came to me: 'The light shines in the darkness, and the darkness can never quite overcome it.'

I am sure I saw God that night.

I think of that story often when I say you find God in the hells of the world. It's where there is nothing but love. The awfulness may be going on, the dreadful cruel awfulness may be going on, but if you look hard enough in that situation, you will find God. You will find the love of God is still there somewhere.

I know that in the Holocaust and times when terrible genocide happens, there can be seen to be no God. But the God of all creation is there keeping the light alive. That is why I'm not afraid to visit the worst hells on earth because that is where God is.

*

At the Wayside Chapel I worked with the poorest of the poor. I was intimately involved with runaway kids, failed adoptions, mothers who'd had their babies ripped from them, kids who had no idea who their parents were and others in all sorts of predicaments. All the time I tried to be true to that Voice. I described myself as a dreamer as a kid. I had always been looking for something different from what I grew up with, because I knew it didn't have to be that way. I was looking for freedom from being told what to be. The Wayside really liberated me – to be and do.

Among other things, I helped establish the Wayside Chapel crisis centre, which worked face to face with the problems of Kings Cross. Together with Ted Noffs I established Life Education centres to provide preventative health education to young people. I was involved with troubled US Vietnam-based soldiers on R&R, I witnessed the explosion of the drug problems at the Cross and God knows what else.

Kings Cross had always been a mecca for gay and transgender people. During that time I heard stories that gay people were undergoing all sorts of indignities to force them to be straight. Transgender people had a very difficult time too. Roberta Perkins, a well-known transgender activist and academic, came to visit me and, after talking, we established classes for males who had undergone transgender therapy. They needed to learn how to behave more like women. To be honest, I didn't expect many to attend these classes, but they were always full. I well remember conservative politician Reverend Fred Nile saying I was doing the work of the devil.

By 1983, however, I knew I was done, and though it was heart-wrenching, it was time for me to leave the Wayside Chapel. I sadly farewelled all the beautiful homeless, helpless and hapless people who had become my extended family in Kings Cross, the square mile or two of Sydney I will always love.

It wasn't a decision taken easily or lightly. Ted and I got on famously. In many ways he was the innovator and frontman and I was the doer, the one who ran the crisis centre and all the other programs. So while, for example, Ted had seen first-hand how health and social issues were affecting the lives of Australian children, I was the one deputised to travel to the US to study programs there and work out how we could set up our own centres. Together with Ted and Barry Masters, an architectural modelmaker, I then drew up the plans for the first Life Education centres. I had already developed the idea of Harold the Giraffe, an education tool to help children learn about health and safety, who is still going strong today as Healthy Harold.

Next I went out into the community and raised funding and got us the grants that enabled Ted to really kickstart Life Education – and things took off. Ted's family became involved: his brother was making the caravans that would take the Life Education program to primary schools around New South Wales and his son was running some of the program. I began to get the feeling I was a bit in the way and I came to the conclusion that, however close Ted and I were, I'd reached as far as I could reach.

*

So I knew my time was up, and I thought, what am I going to do? Ted had encouraged me to really get involved at the Chapel. If Ted was away I would run the meetings. I'd become a registered celebrant, so I could conduct weddings and funerals in Ted's absence. I'd been looking at different religions and spiritual paths. I'd been caught up with the Hare Krishnas and the Children of God, and was gradually transitioning from the secular into the religious life. For years people had suggested I become a lay preacher and work with Ted, but something told me that my future might lie in a different, more spiritual, direction.

I really wanted to continue to work with people. With those in need. But not as a social worker. So I joined the Church and made up my mind to go to theological college. Everyone said, Bill, they'll change you, they'll narrow you, especially after your work with unconventional, sometimes controversial Ted, but I found it was exactly the opposite. There was a breadth and depth of thinking in theology that allowed me to blossom, and the United Theological College in North Parramatta was full of the most accepting staff you could imagine. Being there was fantastic. It was 1983 and I was thirty-nine.

I remember the first time I went to college I freaked, because I turned up in jeans and long hair and there were all these dudes in shorts and long socks. I thought, what have I done? I'd come from the Cross, but I might as well have come from Woodstock or Greenwich Village. The college teachers, administrators and students knew that I'd come from the wayward streets of the inner city, the badlands, but it didn't bother them at all, they didn't treat me differently to anyone else.

Something else that set me apart from the other students was that I had no money, even though I was paid a small stipend to study, which was the reason I had joined the Uniting Church. So I had to do all the assigned and suggested reading in the library because I couldn't afford to buy the books. Gill and I and the family lived in Mortdale, in an old minister's house the Uniting Church rented to us. But we literally did not know how we were going to pay our bills. We were really in debt and struggling.

Then, once again, the Voice spoke. This time I was sitting in my car in a traffic jam, wondering where I was going to find money for petrol and food. All of a sudden everything went still and I felt myself relaxing. I felt a calmness come over me. The Voice had returned to tell me everything would be all right. A couple of days later I found a wad of notes stuffed in my letterbox, totalling well over $800. There was no letter, just the money in an envelope. We *would* be all right! Years later I found out that one of my co-students knew how difficult life was for us. He knew the worry I was experiencing. He had just received his superannuation payout and it was more than he'd expected. He left the excess in my letterbox. He had a totally different theology to mine and we argued a lot. Nevertheless, he gave me the money and I will always be grateful. His generosity of spirit was typical of everyone I encountered at college.

*

'Faith.' What does that even mean? As I've already suggested I think it means trust. Open up any dictionary and the number one definition is 'reliance or trust'. I agree. I've learned enough about Jesus to know that there's more to that man than anyone knows, and I've learned that you can put your trust, whatever that means, in Him.

I sometimes entertain the thought of walking away from the Church, but I know deep down that I can't. I've especially rolled that idea around when times have been tough and the Church has been on my back. I understand why people walk away from their 'professional faith' but not their 'personal faith'. So even if I were to walk away from the Church, I wouldn't ever walk away from my faith. I've had the conversation – I don't know how many times – with people who are going through terrible struggles, who say faith is all bullshit. I just sit with them. They're allowed to think that.

What Jesus would say to them would be: work on forgiving, work on being bigger than whoever or whatever has wronged you, work on not looking for someone to rescue you, work on growing, work on being the best person you can be. That means you've got to face your own anger and throw it away. And then work on finding a group of people who will sit with you.

Easy to say, to write, but it's really hard to do. It's radically hard and that's what Jesus was on about, and that's why I think Pontius Pilate was caught between executing Him or not, because he didn't see Him as a threat to the military. He wasn't, but He was a huge threat to individuals, because He was telling them to turn their lives around.

The idea that God's up in the sky and all-powerful drives me nuts, which I think is the last thing people expect to hear from someone like me. The nature of God is a big battle within Christianity, between the generally more conservative elements who believe in a transcendent, all-powerful God up in heaven and the more progressive elements who believe in an immanent God residing in all living things. Of course there are many views within those ends of the spectrum. As I see it, God cannot be all-loving because so many dreadful things take place. And if God is all-loving, God cannot be all-powerful or He would ensure that everybody was safe and happy. I live with the contradictions of religion. I have experienced many miracles that have felt guided by an outside source and yet feel that God is in the relationships between people. Why would God put $800 in my letterbox and not do the same for everybody else, for example? I don't know and it irritates me that I don't know. The best I can come up with is that not having the answer teaches me to live in the unknowing, to just trust, to have faith.

That higher power, or God, should be able to be explained in a way that is not limited as just Christian or Buddhist or Jewish or Islamic. It's just there. It doesn't need a name, and the more you push into the future or the more you push into the universe, the more it comes back and gives to you.

I say this all the time. I share it from the pulpit, or at least a version of it. I don't say, 'All this big daddy in the sky stuff is rubbish,' as there are people in my congregation who believe in that; instead I try to concentrate on the here and now and God as a loving presence, which is what I believe. God is in loving, compassionate relationships. God is in the mess of life, loving us anyway. I'm learning to live in this conflicted situation and trust that for me and the congregation it will be all right. It's all about finding your own way to God and your own growth in love and compassion, and that is what I try to encourage.

*

Theological college was the making of me. For a start, it opened me up to philosophy. I remember somebody brought up reincarnation, and I said I'd seen things that I couldn't explain any other way. The lecturer, who was the head of philosophy, explained that some of the early followers of Jesus believed He was Elijah reincarnated. His point was that there wasn't a definite answer and that we shouldn't bluntly assert our belief or otherwise in something, we should investigate it. I kept waiting to be told how to think, as so many people had warned me would happen, but instead I was told to think for myself.

College was a place where I had time to explore ideas, and was encouraged to. I wrote a paper there that looked at the street kids of Kings Cross, comparing their plight to something that had taken place 250 years earlier.

In the eighteenth century, there was a royal commission in England into the prison system. Prisoners were being held in hulks moored on the Thames – Magwitch escaped from one in *Great Expectations*. There were people in shackles on those hulks because they'd stolen a loaf of bread to feed their starving children. The stories in the report brought to mind the street kids I'd known in the Cross. Even today a kid can be jailed for stealing a McDonald's chip! One McDonald's chip. We've come nowhere. So I wrote a paper saying there was no difference between the convicts who made this country and the kids on the streets in the 1980s. I was able to give example after example. I'd take my stories from the Cross and overlay them with the stories from the royal commission in 1740 and they would match up.

I was a thorough and enthusiastic student. I've always loved learning. But I did not enjoy the lectures on writing sermons. The lecturers would tell us to spend a couple of days gathering our thoughts and information before drafting a sermon. I'd wonder why I couldn't instead write a sermon on the stuff that happened to me and others every day. The lecturers would assure me that wouldn't be feasible. Perhaps they couldn't come to grips with the stuff I'd seen at the Wayside. Nor could they comprehend that I preferred to leave the sermon writing until the day of its delivery.

Nevertheless, as a good student, I used to read book after book in preparation for a sermon and all I'd deliver was regurgitated twaddle with a few of my own stories thrown in. Until one day I thought that if I really believed in what I wanted to say, I would be able to say it much more convincingly and compellingly if I didn't spout something second-hand from a book. So now I read a couple of things, get a couple of ideas, and then I go from there. Whatever comes, comes.

Even so, when I preach, there's always an inner voice judging me like my father did. Yet whenever I say something that my judging voice reacts to negatively – how dare you say that sort of thing! – I guarantee that someone in the congregation will approach me afterwards to say thank you, that really helped me. I've noticed, since I began speaking more from the heart, that the congregation numbers are increasing, because what I talk about is the here and now, and how the here and now is eternal yet immediate at the same time. In the same way, at any given moment, I feel like half my head's in heaven, whatever that means. I'm always multitasking between two worlds. I take inspiration wherever and whenever I can.

*

College lasted a couple of years. I got on well with my fellow students and the lecturers.

Though I'd already had my brand of spirituality forged in the Cross, I wanted to fit in, I wanted to toe the line, and worked hard to do so. I was always worried I'd spin out of control, so I was careful to listen to the voices of reason the college was so rich in. I wanted to avoid being tarred with the same brush as poor Ted, who'd by then been charged with heresy by the Methodist Church – this was in the 1980s, not the 1600s! I was worried that they might whisper in the cloisters, *he's* one of them.

I saw the stress the heresy charge put Ted under and the emotional toll that fighting and beating it took on him. I could see that it would be a very tricky tightrope to walk, pursuing an active, open, caring ministry like Ted did while maintaining a place within the fold of the Church. My whole life since college has been about walking this difficult tightrope.

There was a price to pay for toeing the line. I had to trade in the bohemian lifestyle. I lost that. I lost my community. I couldn't go back to the Cross for two or three years, because it was so painful.

Just before I completed college, I heard that Cliffy, my homeless Aboriginal comforter and comrade from the steps outside the Wayside, had died. I can never repay him for what he did for me. He's buried somewhere in Penrith in a pauper's grave and I can't find out where he is. 'Paupers' are buried in nameless lots of twelve and that's it. Even if you're a close relative you can't find the exact grave site of a loved one or put a marker on the grave.

This is the kind of thing where real people in need don't

get a look-in. I took up the fight to find Cliffy's grave for a while, but it was futile. But I'll always remember what a beautiful person Cliff was. Compare his compassion with what the minister did on the night of Bob's death. And yet that minister would have looked down his nose at Cliff. One gave life and one gave nothing.

I've found that there are lots of Aboriginal people who give, like Cliff did. We took a group of problem non-Indigenous kids into the bush to meet with some Aboriginal elders and it opened the kids to a spirituality within themselves that they hadn't recognised. Those kids really settled. My gratitude to Cliff for his loving compassion in sitting with me that night can never be repaid to him. So my way of repaying him is to do all that I can for our Indigenous brothers and sisters everywhere. In other words, I universalise my thanks.

*

I graduated in 1986 with a theology degree from Sydney University and was ordained as a minister of the Uniting Church. The Moderator asked me if I wanted to be sent somewhere easy or hard. Life already had me opting for the difficult route every time, so naturally I said 'hard'. He said, 'There's troubles in Ashfield,' and I just knew that was where I had to go. It was as if the Voice itself told me to go there.

RULE #5

Mentor others. That moves what you've learned from your head to your heart and helps others, too.

Many people are on the hunt for someone to mentor them, more often than not in business. But mentoring and being a mentor are not exclusive to that world.

I believe that if I learn something, I should pass it on, freely. I shouldn't clutch hold of it. I can't be like the Dead Sea where the water flows in and then just sits there. Knowledge, experience and information have to flow in and out like the water in the Red Sea does, from the Gulf of Suez in the north to the Gulf of Aden in the south. I try to be a Red Sea by sharing what I've learned.

There have been a lot of mentors in my life, but as often as not I've floundered around on my own and I've always hoped that somebody would take my hand and lead me forward. So I know the value of a good mentor, and the best of all for me was Ted Noffs.

Ted didn't mentor in a traditional way, but if you watched him you learned from the way he behaved. He showed me that it was important to have a good relationship with everybody. On a business level he taught me to sign everything, and to make sure I knew what I was signing. I even learned what not to do from watching Ted: he could sometimes seem like a condemning parent, saying you didn't do this right, you didn't do that right. I learned to watch what he did closely, evaluate it and work out whether it was right for me or not.

Today I write the parish newsletters and I sign all the receipts and have a lot of contact with the people who support us. It's important to look after them. And it's important that I look after them personally.

A little while ago I sent out a couple of birthday cards to some of our volunteers and the response I got was really positive. So now every volunteer gets a card on their birthday and I sign them myself; it builds and strengthens the relationship.

It's the same with our donors; I personally sign the receipts and if I know the donor has something going on in their life, I'll write a quick note: Sorry to hear about Fred, or Congratulations on your promotion, or whatever is appropriate. There are people who give us money who live abroad and I'll find out where they're working and I'll ask them how things are going – it builds that pastoral relationship which is so vital and important. It's easy to look upon donors as nothing but sources of money, and of course they're not, they're living human beings.

I always try to give people respect. And I've put processes in place with my team so they always give people respect too. If somebody rings in, the team member must talk with them respectfully, and try to find out their story so we can do what's best for them. Not everyone instinctively understands that, but by putting processes in place I hope I'm mentoring the volunteers to better relate to those we can help and those who can help us.

Sometimes mentoring can seem quite passive. I learned from Cliffy, my accidental mentor, that if you just sit with someone, just be with them and listen, without criticising or giving unsolicited advice, that can be the gift and assistance a person needs. So much of the mentoring I do now is actually that: sitting and listening or simply being with people.

*

Thomas Merton was an American Trappist monk, a prolific writer, revered theologian, mystic, poet, social activist and ordained priest. My attraction to him took a long time. When I was studying, a theologian I read called Henri Nouwen used to quote Merton a lot, and I'd dipped into his work a bit. Then Gill bought me a book of his as a Christmas present and there's a part in it where he talks about being on a street corner and suddenly everything became one in a loving way, and I recognised that.

If I was hosting one of those imaginary dinner parties where I could invite anyone, Merton would be one of my guests. As a lofty intellectual he would be very different to me, as I sometimes think that people can get lost in what they write, ending up with nothing but words. I'm essentially a very pragmatic person. I have knowledge, some wisdom, a little philosophy – but I have to do something with all that. It's obvious to anyone who knows me that I'm a very 'doing' human being.

Intellectual people can get so caught up in reading and studying that life becomes a series of quotes from other people. They understand the woes of the world and the theory of spirituality, but perhaps they don't appreciate the depth of it. I don't think life's meant to be lived in an ivory tower, contemplating your navel, because the needs of society can be overlooked.

What attracts me to Merton, though, and why I'd love to host him at dinner, is his spectacular brokenness; this man struggled. He had a shiny halo, but without question he had the biggest feet of clay. He was caught up in the mystery of God and faith, and believed strongly in social justice and campaigned fiercely for it, but spent much of his life cloistered away in a monastery. I get annoyed with him and yet I'm interested in him, a man who experienced visions, a man who believed that the one great truth was to live as a child of God in peace with all one's brothers and sisters, with all humanity. Merton knew that social justice was an integral part of that. But perhaps what Merton, who continually strove for self-knowledge, most helped me realise is that the search for God is the search for yourself.

It's never struck me until now that the word 'mentor' is an anagram of Merton.

*

I think Webster was a mentor to me too, a big one. I really loved him in a way that I can't explain. I used to drive him home from the Chapel after Question Time and he'd say, Bill, get out of welfare and get into talking, but I always felt my job was working with people and sitting with people. To be able to look after him when he was dying was a real honour for me. He was down in Scottsdale Hospital in north-east Tasmania. He'd gone to Tasmania thinking that'd be the new Eden and he attracted a lot of followers there. He'd sing all these raucous IRA songs when I was caring for him; they'd echo all through the hospital. He was ninety-something when he died. What I got from Webster was to go out in life and embrace it.

Webster on his ladder at Speakers' Corner in the Domain, 1974.
(© David Barnes)

I oversaw his funeral in Tasmania and wanted to send his ashes to his family in England, but they didn't want them because he'd been such a rebel. So I decided to scatter them in the Sydney Domain, at Speakers' Corner. The Domain said it would cost $20,000, so I went out at midnight, with an ABC news crew, which Webster would have appreciated, and we scattered his ashes all over the Domain for free.

My big thing now is: what to do in the time I've got left? What do I do with all I've learned? I don't want to end up like Merton; I don't want to end up an iconic sage if I can't do things, be helpful, be a force for change. I need a mentor for the remaining years of my life and I haven't found one so far. I hope somebody's going to come along. I need to honour all those people I've known and experiences I've had and I think the way is to do my best to show people that beneath all the terrible difficulties of this life there's something really beautiful. I just don't know how to *do* that, particularly when our country and the world are so lacking in inspirational leadership.

What am I looking for in leadership? I think leaders in the Western world need to not just understand but feel our collective pain. To not be afraid of that pain and actually be able to sit with us in it and lead us through it. We need leaders who understand our sense of increasing isolation and lead us into reconnecting with each other, showing us we can build trust in each other and helping us build our neighbourhoods into communities. We need leaders not to treat us as economic units but as members of a society. We need leaders who are not afraid to tackle the growing inequality by taking on the growing power of multinational corporations, leaders who understand that the larger the organisation, the more amoral it becomes. We need leaders who are not afraid to invest in new industries that will soak up those whose jobs have been lost by increasing automation and artificial intelligence. We need leaders who will make us feel the world will be a better place for our children and grandchildren; thus we need leaders who recognise and celebrate difference, whether individually or culturally, and can also verbalise our collective need to feel part of nature. We know that our natural world is something to cherish rather than exploit or conquer. We need leaders who believe in the goodness of individuals and communities and so build cooperation and respect. If we find leaders like that all the rest will fall into place.

And I will have found my mentor.

CHAPTER SIX

THE TROUBLES AT ASHFIELD

The first time I came to Ashfield Uniting Church, just for a recce, I saw it was a mess, confirming that my post would definitely be a 'hard' one. But if I was to be true to the Voice, I needed to help those most in need, to live on the edge of vulnerability.

The parish was looking for a go-ahead minister, but I was warned that there were those in the congregation who wanted change and those who didn't. I'd need to win over those who weren't particularly keen on change.

So I was very concerned about the interview I had to have with the Ashfield Uniting Church elders. Coming from a 'heretical' Wayside Chapel background, I expected tough theological questioning. After two hours of discussion, mainly about money and membership, I said to them, 'You haven't asked me one theological question.' The eldest of the elders, a well-respected man in his mid-eighties, broke into a sweat. 'You believe in God, don't you?' he asked me. 'Yes,' I answered. 'Well, that's all we want to know,' he said. Questions over. Just like the warnings I'd been given before going to college, the alarm bells that had been sounded with regard to the elders never struck a chord with me.

That first year at Ashfield Uniting Church was difficult and the more conservative members of the congregation ended up leaving. But most people stayed, including a group of ten 'old gals' who were the backbone of the place. Based on my Wayside Chapel experience, I opened the doors and waited for people to come in. The aim was to see what needs they had and whether there was anything I could do to help.

I began by establishing a couple of groups; one was for lonely people to find friends to go out with. Many people are lonely because they find it too difficult to go out alone and meet people. By giving them someone to go out with, they could find additional friends and acquaintances. I also established Uniting Families for the parents and families of addicts who had died. These two groups were really successful, but it was the Uniting Families group that imprinted on my soul as week upon week a new family whose loved child had died of a drug overdose would join us. In these kinds of groups you can't have a week-by-week structure because of the way new people are always joining. It is always day one. This group is still going strong and has morphed into an organisation called Family Drug Support.

I also began a group for parents of children who had suicided. Like the drug parents group, there was always a new grieving parent adding to our numbers every week. I vividly remember one crying mother telling me about the look on her son's face as he was running to jump off the cliff.

'Bill, he had the look on his face like he was running into God's arms.'

Our very first volunteer was David Street, an extremely gentle, timid member of our congregation. Day after day he would sit in the church ready to talk to anyone who turned up. With shaking hands he would make them a cup of tea. 'I'm doing this for God, you know,' he would earnestly tell our visitors. Nowadays we have hundreds of volunteers and I can honestly say that the work they have done has been life-saving for many people.

In that first year I was told by some in the congregation that nothing much happens in Ashfield, and warned by elements of the Church hierarchy not to try to bring Kings Cross to Ashfield. I was keen to find out for myself so used to spend a lot of time on the streets, watching and learning about the neighbourhood, and I also went out with ambulances at night. I discovered that Ashfield could be pretty nasty.

During my walks I'd introduce myself to people I came across and would poke my nose in all sorts of places in an effort to get to know my parishioners. On one such excursion I walked up a flight of stairs in a row of shops, not knowing what I might find at the top. There turned out to be a big table with a group of Italian men playing poker. (Ashfield was largely an Italian and Greek area then.) It was as if I'd strolled onto the set of *Goodfellas*. On the table were hundreds and hundreds, if not thousands, of dollars.

I became a regular visitor to the poker game, though never a participant, and got to know the players a bit. One day the guys were playing poker as usual, with piles of money in the pot, and one of them asked me if I had any kids. I told him I had three and we chatted away and I told him that Michael, a teenager at the time, wanted me to put some money on the Melbourne Cup for him. My newfound friend, whose chair was tilted back on two legs as he chewed on the end of his cigar, folded his cards – snap! – righted his chair, looked me straight in the eye and said, 'I would never fucking agree to any fucking kid of mine being fucking allowed to fucking gamble.' I was stunned by his blatant hypocrisy but thought it best not to point this out. He and I went on to become really good mates. He ran a pizza shop in Leichhardt and used to walk every day from Ashfield to Leichhardt to his pizza shop.

To learn more about the parish I recruited some students to prepare a social profile of Ashfield. We found it was the third most multicultural suburb in Australia at the time, because it's right on the railway line and the migratory waves of people had rolled in on that line from Central Station, one culture, one ethnicity, after another. The old gals didn't know any of that; they thought Ashfield was still Anglo-centric like it had been back in the 1930s; they hadn't seen what I was seeing.

Of course, Ashfield's changed a lot. It was Greek and Italian then and later it was Middle Eastern. All the shops changed overnight from Greek vegetable shops to Lebanese kebab shops, from pizza to pitta. Once upon a time you used to be able to get fish and chips all the way up the main street; there are no places for that now. People come here fresh off the plane, they get a flat here, they make their money and then they go out to somewhere more suburban like the Hills district. So there's never a flourishing Rotary Club or the like in Ashfield because everybody's too busy making money so they can move on. This is a migratory area and I sometimes think that many of the shop-owners and retailers at Ashfield could well be the friends I'd made when I lived near there as a kid, only now all grown up. I can't imagine that they would have recognised me as the English–Aussie kid they'd kicked around with in the bush at the back of St Marys.

The community's a great deal more Asian today. And there are probably a lot more mental health issues now. Paradoxically, I think the Cross has changed to be more like the Ashfield of old – and Ashfield's changed to be more like the Cross.

There was a transvestite who belonged to our congregation. As a male he was Ian and as a female she was Ina – a simple rearrangement of letters to match the changeable identities. Ina played the piano really well and knew all the hymns and the old gals loved her. They'd sit around the piano singing and they never knew Ina was Ian. In truth, I didn't see much difference here to the Cross: it was just as colourful, just as unpredictable. In Ashfield, though, I didn't have Ted as a backstop: everything began and ended with me.

*

We'd only just moved into the manse – the house at the back of the church – and there was a knock at the door. A lot of people used to knock on the door for money, but this time a couple were standing there and asked if they could come in, which wasn't usually the case. I let them in, then thought what a mug I'd been as they were probably about to rob me. How wrong can you be? They looked at me and said, will you marry us? Even though I was taken aback, I was grateful that I wasn't fighting for my life and said of course.

The woman's husband had died climbing Mount Kilimanjaro, the man's wife had left him, and this couple had found each other among the ruins of their relationships. The woman cried when I said yes. They'd been knocked back by their Catholic priest who'd given them a huge blast and lectured them on the immorality of living in sin, all of that codswallop.

My mind flashed back to another minister's residence not so very far away, not so many years earlier, when cold comfort was all that was on offer to me when I'd gone looking for charity in the old sense of the word – the love of humankind – and come away empty-handed. It was lovely to balance things out.

Things like that would happen all the time. There'd be people with end-of-line issues: they'd been to churches or to counsellors and received nothing, so they ended up at Ashfield. I learned that you just respond to the human need.

I was determined that Ashfield Uniting Church would be a place where people were welcome, a place of sanctuary, a place where if I'd turned up as a young person whose brother had been killed, I wouldn't be turned away. I wanted to make sure that no one left feeling worse than when they came in, and preferably feeling a whole lot better.

*

Ashfield Uniting Church was so poor there wasn't even money for stamps and I realised that if I was to achieve anything I had to find financial supporters. To do this, I needed to cultivate a profile, just as Ted had at the Wayside, so I started putting stories in the local paper, particularly about the people who were coming to the church for help – which actually brought more people seeking help to our door! I persisted, because I really wanted to open the place up, despite suspecting that the Church hierarchy would not approve. (In my experience, the most successful people in the Church are often those who do the least but talk the talk. That's not me, it's not in one atom of my DNA.) I became good friends with one of the journalists, who used to run a story almost every week. Every night I'd walk our dog around the neighbourhood, taking my Dictaphone, gathering stories of people in need who I encountered.

Someone I hoped would help was John Singleton, who'd built his wealth and success in advertising. I decided to contact him.

Meanwhile more and more people were dropping in to the church at all hours, and I realised many of them were simply hungry. So we'd scrape together whatever money we had and on Monday night we'd buy a leg of lamb to cook for those who came in need. Pretty soon quite a few people were turning up and our resources were really stretched. Fortunately, people have an uncanny knack of appearing in my life just when I need them most, as was the case when a young man called Rob appeared one Monday. Rob was a really good cook and was happy to throw his lot and talents in with us. Word got around, and even more hungry people started to come to our Monday night roasts, which soon went by the name of 'Rob's Kitchen'. We were struggling to cope with the demand when help materialised and in the most unexpected fashion, even if I'd been the one who'd set the ball rolling.

*

My relationship with Singo (John Singleton) began way back around 1970. He and I became mates through Ted. One of the best debates I ever heard was between John and Jack Mundey, a union leader and environmental activist who led the fight against the property development in the Cross and other parts of Sydney. It was Question Time at the Wayside Chapel, around 1972. John and Jack were ferocious but friendly in their verbal to-ing and fro-ing about the future of Australia. They both wanted a better Australia but diverged on how to get there: freedom versus collectivism. The two of them – Mundey and Singleton – became great mates after that.

Some of my own best debates have been with John too. We discuss religion passionately but amicably. I think he is attracted to it but doesn't feel good enough. I well remember sitting with him in the church one say and him saying to me, 'God could never love me, Bill.' I answered, 'John, do you know about King David?' I was sure he did but I told him the story anyway – how King David had all these women but then he wanted this special one who was already married. So he organised for her husband to be killed during a war-time exercise so that he could have her as his wife instead.

'John,' I said, 'God loved King David more than anyone. And if God loved King David, he can love you.'

'Ah no, Bill,' John said, 'God could never love me.'

John is wealthy, but people don't become millionaires by giving their money away. A lot of them are mean bastards, but not Singo: he gives. He will give away a million dollars, just like that, if the cause is good and true – and there are very few people like that. He said to me once that there was little, if anything, that separated him from my customers: he'd been in prison and a tearaway and knew that he could easily have fallen the other side of the line.

When Ted got sick, John and another Australian entrepreneur, Dick Smith, paid all Ted's medical bills, which must have cost a fortune. Dick Smith is another who doesn't hesitate to put his hand in his pocket for a good cause. I remember him giving me a cheque for five grand in the Wayside days, just because he liked the work I was doing. Of course I passed it on to Ted, who swiftly contacted Dick and managed to extract even more money for the Life Education centres.

But back to my money difficulties at Ashfield. One Saturday morning, very early, there was a knock on my door and it was Singo. I think he had a Rolls Royce at the time, which was parked outside. I invited him in, we sat down and

Singo and me in the Loaves & Fishes Free Restaurant in 1990.

he put a small hessian sack on the table. He looked at me through bleary eyes – who knows if he'd been up all night – nodded in the direction of the sack and said, 'I've just won all this money on a horse of mine, what would you do if I gave it to you?' I didn't have to think twice. I told him I'd open a soup kitchen. He thought for a second, said fine and pushed the bag towards me. 'Call it Loaves & Fishes,' he said. He gave me all the money in the sack and emptied out every pocket he had, all full of cash; he just kept piling it up.

Initially we ran Loaves & Fishes Free Restaurant from an old Boy Scout hall across from our church, as I didn't want to startle my old gals too much by operating from the church hall from the get-go. (I knew, though, that once the congregation saw that those coming to the restaurant were simply hungry people and not criminals they would happily recommend that we move Loaves & Fishes into our church hall.) We opened on the Monday after Singo's visit and got help from other generous people too. The local mayor, Lew Herman, donated all the pots and pans and another councillor donated money. Another flamboyant millionaire mate, Rene Rivkin, good-humouredly opened the place; he was as much at home with all the down-and-outs as with the rich people in Sydney.

We did all the cooking up at the church, then wheeled the food down to the scout hall in shopping trolleys. Within six months we were set up in the church hall, as I'd hoped and expected, seating eighty to ninety people a day. It was chaos, but organised chaos, and it's still going on.

*

Contrary to popular belief, chaos is not an environment in which I thrive, but I acknowledge that life is messy. I sometimes think that if it's not messy, it's not real.

I found this prayer recently:

Disturb us Lord, when we are too well-pleased with
ourselves,
when our dreams have come true because we have
dreamed too little,
when we arrive safely because we have sailed too close to
the shore.
Disturb us Lord, when with the abundance of things we
possess,
we have lost our thirst for the waters of life.
Having fallen in love with life,
we have ceased to dream of eternity
and in our efforts to build a new earth
we have allowed our vision of the new heaven to dim.
Disturb us Lord, to dare more boldly
to venture on wider seas

where storms will show your mastery
where losing sight of land, we shall find the stars.
We ask you to push back the horizons of our hope
and to push into the future
in strength, courage, hope and love.

That prayer, written around 1577, is ascribed to Sir Francis Drake, famous for repelling the Spanish Armada as it attempted to invade England. I heartily endorse its sentiments. I've always said that if you believe you've been 'saved' by God, you definitely haven't been: being saved is not something to achieve, it's something to work towards. Christians who believe they're 'saved' tend to think that they don't have to do anything; they can sit back smugly and pay lip service to God, who will do it all for them. They need to be disturbed! I invite and encourage them – and everyone – to use Sir Francis Drake's prayer, to pray to be disturbed. Actually I think we are always being disturbed. It depends whether we listen or not. Chaos can prompt us to spread our wings and soar.

*

If a bag of horse-racing money was the birth certificate of Loaves & Fishes, then the Exodus Foundation was midwifed in an equally extraordinary way.

About the same time as Singo handed me a sack of cash, I met Graham Williams, who was a reporter at the *Sydney Morning Herald*. He got into lots of trouble with me or, should I say, through me.

French newspapers at the time were looking for dirt on Australia to counteract the blowback France was getting because of the country's nuclear testing in the South Pacific. The French press did some digging and thought maybe they could write about the way Australia treated its homeless, the sort of people we look after here and I'd had so much to do with at the Wayside. A French correspondent got in touch with me and together we talked to the lord mayor of Sydney and his wife, who claimed to be doing a lot of work with homeless kids. I contacted Graham and with a photographer from the *Herald* we went out one night and found a big group of homeless kids sleeping rough on the back steps of the Sydney Town Hall. We took photos and Graham wrote a story about the rubbish the mayor was peddling, claiming he was doing a lot to help the homeless. It was a good story, with a good photo, captioned 'Sydney's Shame'.

When the story broke, and people figured out I was behind it, the local government officials responsible for caring for the homeless went looking for dirt on me; they really wanted to destroy me. That didn't happen, but Graham got booted out of the *Herald*, maybe for that story, maybe for others he'd run with my help that shone light on other areas where our councils and politicians had been failing us.

Because of my familiarity with the issue, I had been asked to give evidence to the National Inquiry into Youth Homelessness, chaired by Brian Burdekin, the Federal Human Rights Commissioner. Brian told me there were lots of homeless kids around Central Railway Station, so I decided to go and see. I got there at midnight and talked to the railway police. They told me there'd be at least fifteen kids sleeping rough there every night, and the New South Wales police told me they could find at least fifteen others every night too. From that day, the police brought any homeless kids they could round up to Ashfield. We had nothing in the way of bedding or accommodation, so I used to 'crash' them in the pews of the church, in the vestry and in the church hall. The numbers were building up and I put out more stories about the kids, and asked for volunteers to help.

Help duly arrived again, this time via an Australia Post delivery.

A little old lady sent me a letter in which she wrote, 'This is for the lovely homeless children you're looking after. You are not to send me a receipt or to ring me or to contact me in any way because when my family find out they'll be very angry with me.' Another slip of paper fluttered out of the envelope: it was a cheque for $10,000. This was in the late

1980s, so God knows what it'd be worth today. I thought, jeez, if I was crooked I could piss off; Bermuda, here I come!

Instead, I established the Exodus Foundation, so-called because Moses led the children of Israel out of their bondage, and I, maybe foolishly, thought that like Moses we'd be leading homeless children out of their plight. Tragically, many of the first crop of homeless young people we took in died, either from drug overdoses or car smashes, and I keenly feel their loss to this day. In many ways a lot of what I do now is aimed at trying to make sure people don't have to suffer like they did.

One of the problems with the homeless kids was that we would get them all scrubbed up so they could go back to school, but the schools couldn't cope with them. Necessity being the mother of invention, we decided to establish our own school. After much searching I came across Professor Kevin Wheldall and the Macquarie University School of Special Education. They had developed a marvellous reading program for children who couldn't read – just like many of the homeless kids. Ultimately, not only did we set up a school for already homeless kids, we developed the Exodus Tutorial Centre programs for those kids who were still at school and at home but were in danger of falling out of both.

As the publicity surrounding my work grew, more people contacted me offering donations of financial and other support. Over the years the number of these kindly souls has continued to increase. Many of them are pensioners who donate perhaps a hundred dollars, and others are quite wealthy. I find myself drawn to all of them. The relationship between us is personal, and in many ways I am a pastor to them, just as much as I am to my congregation and to the homeless and needy I help look after. At times people have tried to exploit my relationship with our donors to get them to increase their donations, and if I've ever been vaguely tempted to allow this to happen I have only to remember what one donor said to me: 'Bill, I'm your friend, not your wallet.' That statement taught me a lot.

Over time we have raised more than $70 million dollars for people in need and I feel we are only just beginning. It's amazing how at the right time food appears, or just the person we're looking for. I think that is because we're here for the poorest of the poor and offer what we have freely and with love.

None of this could have happened without the strong support of our church membership. In those early days the core members of my congregation were those ten greying formerly Methodist ladies who I refer to lovingly as the 'old gals'. They and the rest of the congregation literally took me in, loved me for who I was, accepted me and all the disadvantaged people I brought with me. It turned their lives upside down. I will never now agree with the view that elderly church people are inherently conservative. As one of the old gals told me, 'Bill, we were just a bunch of old fogies going out backwards.' They stood up for me against the negative forces and we all learned a lot along the way. Unlike the more conservative members of my congregation, the old gals weren't surprised to see me leading protests against the Malaysian government to try to stop the hanging of Kevin Barlow and Brian Geoffrey Chambers for drug trafficking. The old gals and I became very close and I vow I will never leave Ashfield until I've buried the last of them. As of today only two of those dear gals remain. Our whole congregation has mourned the passing of the other great ladies. As I continue to say, without their help none of my work would have got off the ground.

*

The old gals and I used to regularly meet with mutual friends at what was loosely called a 'discussion group'. However, it was really a time for us just to share together. I quickly learned that if I shared with them what I was planning to do, whatever I said would miraculously happen. Those times we shared together mean such a lot to me.

One day, they asked me about Islam. So I invited a friend, Sheikh Jihad, to one of these meetings so they could learn about Islam first-hand.

At the duly appointed time, Jihad turned up at the front door and knocked. One old gal opened the door for him and went to shake his hand. He quickly withdrew his hand and said it was inappropriate for him to do something like that. Emboldened, Jihad also said to her that she should have her hair covered because it was the sexiest part of her body.

The old gal would have none of this. 'Darling,' she said, looking him straight in the eye, 'if I should have my hair covered, you should be wearing gloves.' Jihad had long sensitive fingers.

To put it mildly, it was an interesting start to proceedings.

The old gals sat in a circle with Jihad in the middle. They and Jihad gave as good as they got. Suddenly, Jihad looked at his watch and said, 'It's my time to pray.'

Lunch with the 'old gals', the backbone of the Ashfield parish.

I thought, this is going to be interesting. He asked them if he could move into another room. 'No, you can pray right here and now,' they said. He got out his prayer mat and tried to work out the direction of Mecca. One of the old gals who was very bright, said, 'Everyone knows Mecca is in that direction, over our mantelpiece.'

Jihad placed his prayer mat in the right direction and then got down on his knees to pray in the centre of the circle of old gals.

I will never know who said it but someone said, 'A little bit of prayer wouldn't hurt all of us, you know.'

The next moment, while Jihad continued to pray, saying 'Allahu Akbar' and bowing with his forehead to the carpet, the old gals in a circle around him started saying the Lord's Prayer.

It was one of the most moving moments of my life.

Not long after this day, the events of 9/11 took place and the old gals got me to bring Jihad and his family to our church so they would be safe.

*

One Sunday morning something strange happened and everything changed for me. Communion began as usual. However, towards the end of it I began to sense something odd. I kept on intoning the words of the liturgy but became aware of an unexpected presence in the church. It came as a shock to me to realise that the ghostly presence was that of the Reverend Ted Noffs, who'd been dead for several years. As the service progressed there were two conversations going on in my brain, one with Ted and the other with the congregation. What are you doing here, Ted? I asked as I felt his spirit hovering above the organist. He said, Bill, I'm here to say goodbye. I have to go. I was aghast. You can't go, I said. I need you. Who am I going to talk to? Ted's spirit responded, Bill, I've taught you as much as I can. You're on your own now.

I couldn't leave it at that. Don't go, Ted, I begged. Now all this was going on in my head while I was distributing the Communion elements. Don't go Ted, I cried again as I felt his spiritual presence fading. It's time to go. It's up to you now, he said. And he was gone. I was so overcome that at the end of Communion I stood before the congregation and told them word for word what had happened. Then the tears came.

*

In his early sixties, Ted had a stroke that paralysed him. He was going to have one sooner or later because he frantically ran around and was in a constant state of tension. I remember one day he couldn't go to work, he was so uptight. The team got him into the car and drove him to the Wayside, but he couldn't get out of the car, so they drove round and round the block, encouraging him until he got out of the car and got to work. He'd had some sort of breakdown.

After his stroke it was dreadful. I visited him in hospital. He begged me to get him out of the place, and I had to decline. He said, Bill, you're a minister, you can do whatever you like, get me out of here. I had to say no.

I'd seen Ted at the height of his powers: he could walk into a room, any hall large or small, and within minutes everyone would be galvanised into action. I'd also seen Ted at his lowest, when he'd lash out and attack me and others in his team. Yet I stayed loyal. I realised that the most important thing for the second-in-command to be was loyal to whoever was in charge.

When I first came to Ashfield, I had no assistant, no loyal lieutenant, there was nothing here. I had to earn my own salary. When I mentioned the lack of money, even for stamps, the Church asked me who I wanted to write to. There was even a family who came to my door and criticised my sermons. No wonder I thought of Ted and wished for his guidance so often.

For all his earthly charisma and for all of his flaws, Ted had his head in heaven. After that strange Communion, it was time for me to let him go.

*

A number of years ago I was under a lot of stress regarding Exodus. We were short of money and really struggling. We held meetings about how to keep going and I said we weren't going to cut programs. Everything would either sink or swim together.

During this upheaval the mother of one of our volunteers died and he asked me to conduct her funeral. The church was full of people and I can, to this day, see the son's weeping face in the pews. He was the ultimate mother's boy and I must confess that I disliked him. Everything had to be exactly right for the funeral. I don't know why I took this attitude towards him but he somehow irritated me.

In my time I have conducted many funerals and this one was not unusual for me. I knew what to do and what to say. I was at the pulpit, intoning the words of the service, when out of the corner of my right eye I noticed an area of light. It slowly got brighter and clearer and then I noticed a figure within it. For those of you who have seen the hologram of Princess Leia in the *Star Wars* films you will know what I mean. A sort of ghostly figure appeared in the corner of my eye.

All of a sudden I realised who it was: Jesus! The figure stood beside me for what I thought was an age. You've never appeared to me before, I said, I've only sensed your presence; why are you so clear now? Because you're strong enough, He told me. I wanted things to stay like that forever: there was such a lovely feeling of strength and calmness and lovingness in His presence. It was an energising, sustaining, life-giving experience. Meanwhile, I kept going with the funeral. After a while, the image began to fade and, true to form, just as it had been with Ted, I said – in my head – don't go. You'll be fine now was the response.

Those two experiences pushed me to draw on greater depths in myself and also look for other forms of mentoring. I needed mentoring by a leader.

*

As the Ashfield congregation grew, I was confronted by an issue I had never faced before: I began to understand pressures and temptations of the job that were new to me. It is the unspoken reality of the humanness of every minister. We care, we show love and concern, and from that position of power, some clergy have destroyed their ministry. For me, the ministry destroyed my personal relationships. Two failed marriages are ample evidence of that. To be honest, the ministry allowed me to hide, and not show up to the people that mattered most: my partners and my children. It has taken me many years and painful apologies to realise the importance of simply showing up in relationships.

As I said, some clergy are destroyed by their inappropriate desires. I remember one woman coming to our church. A well-known Anglican minister had been regularly having sex with her. She had been to the church hierarchy and they wouldn't do anything for her. In that moment I saw the complete loss of integrity, not just in the minister, but in the system that chose to look away.

I thought, that's one area to keep well out of.

When it comes to sex there is so much hypocrisy in the world, particularly in the church. Respected parishioners and ordained ministers, who are looked up to as pillars of virtue, aren't necessarily so. And as long as appearances are kept up, church hierarchies have for far too long been content to turn a blind eye! It is only now, after such a brutal royal commission into institutional child abuse, that we see a system paying more attention. It is sad to me that it is so hard to simply live a life of honesty and transparency. Why is that so? Why is it that many people, especially 'do-gooders', would rather have hypocrisy?

Maybe this wisdom comes with age but it has taken me a long time to be able to share friendships with women without raising suspicion in others that it is about romance or sex. I say this with great respect to those who find themselves sitting in churches; males in positions of religious authority, in positions of power, are also vulnerable to their own human desires. If a minister gives in to that vulnerability, everybody loses. Not only that, well-intentioned and meaningful work can be destroyed.

Relationships are not easy in this line of work but, truthfully, they are not easy anywhere. However, in my world they can end up on the front pages of the *Daily Telegraph* and it is even worse.

How do I deal with people, if I want to sit beside them and care about them and show compassion? How do I do that when those I am in a relationship with see that I am not showing up with them? Well, what I have learned is that when I privilege this work over the relationship, when I fail to show up, my partners rightfully become edgy and jealous and the relationship becomes doomed.

In reality it has tended to ensure that I am alone more often than I'm not.

The Church has begun to understand the problem. It's more understanding than it used to be. However, any sexual and romantic entanglement can tarnish your ability to be effective. Even though you are only human, you are expected by some parishioners and some donors to be more than human. My fear is that in trying to be more than human, we stumble, and in this work, stumbling is exploitation of another vulnerable person. And that is not ever acceptable. People need to feel safe in a church. People deserve to feel safe in a church and it is so easy for that sense of safety to be breached and trust broken.

I don't think human beings are naturally monogamous. Maybe a few are, but the rest of us have to deal with temptation and questions of integrity all the time. I know a minister who was tossed out of the Church in the days before the administration became a little more sympathetic to real-life problems. He had a big congregation, was happily married and then he met a woman and the two of them fell deeply in love. She left her husband to live with him. He left his wife. They ended up in Kings Cross working for the Wayside. He was really a good counsellor and it was obviously a love match: they were together for thirty-five years; it wasn't just a passing affair.

I married them and sat with him when he died. The Church excommunicated him. If anyone didn't deserve to be excommunicated it was him, yet God knows how many have got away with affairs by hiding them. Hypocrisy and monogamy make bad bedfellows.

Your personal life won't be that happy. That was what the Voice said.

RULE #6

_Do_ who you are. Life is a _doing_ as well as a navel-gazing exercise. If you keep it at the navel-gazing stage, there is no progress.

You'll probably look at this rule and think, right, _do_ who you are? What does that mean? I'll never know the situation you're in right now – you might be riding the subway in New York or lying on a beach in Copacabana – so I can't tell you what to do, but I know that if you actively _do_ things rather than think about them, the situations around you will change. Actions speak much louder than thoughts and prayers. The problem is that thoughts and prayers are easy; action and getting in there is a world away from that.

I remember when Bill (William) Deane was Governor-General of Australia. In 1999 he attended a memorial service in Switzerland for fourteen Australian kids who died when they were swept away in a flash flood. Deane and his wife took fourteen sprigs of wattle with them, stood with and comforted the families where the kids had died, and said they were bringing a little bit of Australia to the kids, which

124

meant so much to those left behind. That was leadership, and that was doing. I think too about our former prime minister John Howard and his swift actions following the Port Arthur massacre to seriously tighten gun laws nationally. So much better for the country than thoughts and prayers.

It's in the hells you find heaven, because the experience you get in those places is genuine. It's where life is right on the edge. You might find heaven for a moment while singing a hymn in church, but for it to last you have to *do* it. If you're talking about the dispossessed, you have to *do* it, like Bill Deane so often did but that lord mayor of Sydney only pretended to do.

Years ago, at the Wayside Chapel, when we built the first Life Education centre, we used light-emitting diodes to make a star ceiling, and when we turned on the lights for the first time, giving us the feeling that we were looking out into the universe, perhaps into the unknown, an old guy in the audience said to me, Bill, all my life I've said to God I'll dedicate my life to You, just tell me what to do, and every day God has said, not yet Charlie, not yet. Charlie was in his nineties, still waiting, and I thought, crikey Charlie, you should have gone out and just done *something*, and it would have come back to you in spades.

He was similar to that rich, young ruler who came to Jesus and said, what do I have to do? And Jesus said, give up all that you value, but he couldn't do it; most people can't. If, however, you give up all that you value, you will get back something beautiful. Even giving up a little of yourself for others will reward you.

The hope I have for you is that you'll take a risk. For example, I've learned that the more honest I am – the more I *do* honesty – the more people like me. So if you *do* honesty, lovingness or compassion, you and your relationships will change too, for the better.

*

A few years ago, a young man dropped in to see me. 'I know you do work in Africa,' he said. 'I want to work there for you. I can't do it now, but I'll be back.'

Then he told me his story. 'My parents migrated from Italy and worked their butts off in a pizza shop to give me an education. I went to university and ended up running my own building business. In a short time, I had everything. I had the business, the money, the wife, the car, the house, everything. I was living a pretty good life. But I loved to gamble. I got caught up with gambling and, over time, I lost the business, the money, the wife, the car, the house, everything. My addiction took everything.

'I was sitting in a room, all by myself, when I saw a film

about the problems in Africa and just knew I had to go there. So I lied my way into a Christian missionary group and ended up in Kenya. However, the Christian group realised I wasn't a true Christian and they threw me out. I was out on the street, in Kenya, with nothing.

'I realised I had two choices. I could beg for some money to get back to Australia, which could be hard, or I could head further into Africa. I decided to head further into Africa. I ended up in a remote village which had been decimated by AIDS. Most people were either dead, sick or dying. They were just lying around, with no hope or anything.

'At first, I didn't know what to do. But then I realised I could help by teaching them my skills. I got the able-bodied people together and taught them how to make mud bricks. Brick by brick, we built a hospital.

'It was while doing that that I changed. I realised I had to go back to Australia, pay off all my debts and then come back to Africa and help. The hospital is now built and I'm back in Australia, working three jobs to pay off my debts.

'I'll be back to see you when my debts are all paid off because I want to work for you in Africa.'

When I asked him for a phone number, he said he couldn't give me one because Telstra was after him with a phone bill which was pretty big. He said he'd contact me.

When I told this story to a wealthy friend of mine, he said he would pay off the phone bill. However, when I saw the man again and told him about the offer he refused to accept the money, as he had to pay it off himself.

I haven't seen him yet. Maybe he hasn't paid all his debts off yet. Fate has a funny way of changing things. I know one day he'll be back to work with me in Africa.

*

Buddhists say we are like whirlpools in a river; so you've got a whirlpool and I've got a whirlpool but where do you and your whirlpool finish and where do I and mine begin? At what point can you say this is you, not me?

I've often suspected that people think there's some nugget at the heart of every human: a core, the centre of the being, which if they work towards hard enough, they'll get to. There isn't such a thing, it does not exist. Instead, as science tells us, we're all more like a whirlpool or a rope of coiled little fibres – fibres of experiences, DNA and so much more.

So we, as 'individuals', do not strictly exist. When we get together in a group, we're not there as 'individuals', we're all part of something overlapping and bigger. We, as individuals, are pretty small. We can each only hold a gigabyte of memory, so that when you look at 'Bill', for instance, it isn't that much;

most of what makes us function as humans within a society is outside us as individuals, though we help determine what that 'outside' consists of.

This is where the scientist in me and the spiritual side of me meet. We know from atomic physics that the observer has an effect on the observed. The reality we see is only a projection of what's inside us, so if we change inside, everything out there in the world changes too. Act once and you change yourself inside. And if you don't act, if you don't change inside, you're just stagnating and your world is too: you're going nowhere.

I think that Jesus maybe only realised this at His own baptism by John the Baptist; before that He'd been a follower of John, but when He was immersed in the River Jordan all the bells and whistles went off for Him and He realised that what He had to do was work on Himself, turn Himself around, get His act together. He knew that real change would come from within. If He changed Himself within, everything else would change around Him and the world would be a better place. It was really subversive, because an army couldn't touch it; He was saying, look, you guys, get it together, identify what's stuffing up your life, work on it, confess it and move on. By doing so you'll change the world. That was so healing and in a way mountains did move. The Roman Empire thought it could kill Jesus, but it couldn't and didn't. Jesus talked about eternal life, which I think has more to do with the eternal 'now' and how it changes who we are.

*

Years ago I would go into the church and read a sermon that was a mish-mash of other people's thoughts. I'd find out what the topic for the day was, then I'd read up on it, get bits and pieces from different sources, and stand up and say Matthew said this and Peter said that. I was forever preaching someone else's thoughts.

There's nothing more artificial than that. There's nothing as inauthentic as using the thoughts of somebody else, unless you've incorporated them into yourself – and the only way of achieving that is *doing* what you learn. One magnificent day, I realised that it was time to be authentic. That's really hard. It requires courage and being prepared to be vulnerable.

In the past it's been very difficult for me to be genuinely myself around people who want to put me in a box and be what their imaginings are. But as I've already noted I've learned over the years to say, this is me and you walk along beside me or you jump off the bus. I've found that this is not just liberating for me, it's liberating for other people too. I'm not trying to be what somebody else wants me to be, and they are not having to respond to the inauthentic me. We often betray ourselves to keep relationships, and it takes bravery to reveal your true self. Your friends and acquaintances who don't want to change in order to relate to the new you will arc up and try to push you back to the old you they're familiar with. That can be hard to swallow, but I think I've reached the stage where I can resist that now.

*

For many years I was only able to be my authentic self around my psychotherapist, Dr Bob Wotton (every person needs a good shrink), who has been there for me since 1986, and my relationship advisor, Jon Graham. At the time I met Jon, I needed to sort out some issues with a few people at Ashfield. I asked a friend who works in marriage guidance counselling if they had any recommendations for people who might be able to assist me. Of the five names they gave me, I chose to contact Jon simply because his practice was nearby. Once the employment issues and relationships were sorted out he stayed to work with us. I have been so grateful to him for his wisdom and guidance over the years. Once again, a seemingly random choice probably wasn't.

I've also been working on getting my relationship back with my kids. This has been hard as I've had to face my own failings and have had to apologise for my part in their struggles. I'm like Sisyphus rolling the stone up the hill: it keeps rolling back down again, burdened with the things I attempt to do but can't. With my therapist I'm discovering parts of myself that I didn't know existed, but it's taken a long time. The Buddha said that the broken heart is a beautiful thing because it has compassion, and that's true.

Something I'm still trying to work out is how my life was heading in one direction, as an engineer, but then I got a calling and it headed off in a completely different direction. But there's not one part of me that regrets following the call and if I had my life over, I'd do the same. All of it: the good, the bad, the ugly and the indifferent. For it's been a life of *doing*.

CHAPTER SEVEN

BLOOD, COMFORT AND CHRISTMAS

My involvement with the 'tainted blood' scandal and the fight for compensation for the victims started with Gill and the blood transfusion she had before giving birth to Eme. Around the time Tim was born, seven years later, she'd started having problems with her liver. Acupuncture was helping, but not curing her. It wasn't until a few years afterwards that we found out she'd got hepatitis C through that blood transfusion.

Hepatitis C is a virus that affects the liver. It is transmitted through blood-to-blood contact. About 80 per cent of people infected with hepatitis C develop chronic health problems. Without treatment, sufferers can die from liver failure or cancer of the liver.

While trying to come to grips with Gill's diagnosis, I met Charles McKenzie, who'd also contracted hepatitis C through a transfusion, but his had occurred when he was a child. Charles and I decided to form an organisation to pursue justice for people like him and Gill and we invited anyone in similar circumstances to join us for a meeting at Ashfield. I thought that maybe a handful would show up. Hundreds turned up. We had a church full of people.

When people end up here, when they come to me, it's often because they have exhausted all other avenues: no one is listening, they're tired and depleted. We're the end of the line. I was determined to do my best for them.

Gill and I went with a barrister, Anthony Tudehope, to the Red Cross, which had provided the blood for Gill's transfusion. They agreed that Gill had been given blood from a donor who had hepatitis C. They even named him. However, they said there would be no compensation. This wasn't just their response to Gill, one isolated case; they had the same response for everyone, including Charles and all the people who had met with us in the church. All these people were to get nothing and some of them were dying because of the contaminated blood they'd received.

What we discovered was that the head of the blood transfusion service at the Red Cross in Australia, in those early days, wasn't a doctor; he was an aeronautical engineer.

He and his team had known that they were supplying contaminated blood, but took a gamble that the hepatitis C virus, about which not much was known in the early 1970s, was relatively benign, even though the US, Canada and the UK had refused to use blood contaminated by hepatitis C.

Charles and I agitated for a Senate inquiry, which eventually took place in 2004. I knew the wearying path it travelled down: I've been caught up in a lot of these things where stuff just gets pushed below the surface because there'd be too much of a scandal and billions of dollars would need to be paid out. So nothing came of the inquiry. Some victims had fortunately managed to get compensation using legal threats, but had been forced to sign secrecy clauses, preventing them from speaking publicly about what had happened.

ABC TV's *Four Corners* devoted an episode to the tainted blood scandal, but time moves on and other equally urgent matters shout for our attention. It's like climate change. The reality can stare you in the face, but it doesn't mean you have to do anything. That's what I mean when I say you have to do what you are. If you bang on about integrity and trust and honour and all of that, you'd better *do* it. Some people whom we put great trust in don't *do* it; they just bang on about it, and people die.

The Senate inquiry was held in 2004 and it's now 2021. The estimated 10,000 people infected by tainted blood are still waiting for an apology from the federal government, an outcome recommended by that inquiry sixteen years ago. In my heart of hearts I don't think that there will ever be reparation for the victims of the tainted blood scandal. Hundreds turned up to that first meeting in the church, but gradually many of those victims died, and years later, when we held another meeting, only three people turned up. One of them was a former police commissioner. He'd been working on projects in Thailand when he discovered he had hepatitis C and suddenly nobody wanted to know him. He was broken.

People thought I'd be able to move mountains, but only God can do that; all I can do is bring a proverbial shovel and help with the moving. Many thought I'd be able to get publicity and everything would change, but just because you're in the right doesn't mean governments or organisations are going to do anything. But it's not a reason to give up. As John, in his Gospel, says, we can only be signs. Signs that the world *can* be a better place if we all want it to be. That helps me a lot.

I think that some in the hepatitis C group were disappointed in me. The victims and families of the tainted blood scandal *should* be disappointed with the lack of compassion and fairness shown to them, and perhaps I was the only person they could take it out on. I understand, and am grateful, that

Joanne McCarthy, a journalist with the *Newcastle Herald*, is still plugging away at the issue.

It became for me more than just another sadness in the world. Nowadays I still come across children who have become infected with hepatitis C because of their parents' blood transfusions two or three decades earlier. We are now seeing a generational transfer of this disease simply because people unknowingly received tainted blood transfusions and never knew they had to get tests. Their children are now getting sick.

No matter how many stories I get involved with – some with positive outcomes, some not – I think the tainted blood scandal is one of those I will go to my grave feeling really sad about. I wish I could do more.

*

I came across another issue that really moved me when I started at the Wayside Chapel. I got caught up in the issue of newborns that were unwillingly put up for adoption by teenage mothers – kids themselves – who'd been placed under immense pressure by hospitals and homes for mothers and babies to give their babies away. I remember one girl telling me that a social worker had urged her to do the 'right thing', that she was only sixteen and wouldn't have a future with a baby – she should give it up to people who'd love it. She gave the baby up and later asked the same social worker if the baby had gone to a good home. And the social worker turned on her and said, why would you care, you gave it away.

What comfort do you give a teenager like that?

I've got letters from so many people who put their kids up for adoption. There's one that breaks my heart. This guy wrote that he and his girlfriend had a child when they were both sixteen. The baby was adopted, but later he and the mother married and had other children. At all of their birthday parties, they keep a chair empty for the missing member of the family.

The first meetings of former kids in care (Care Leavers Australia) was held in my church. Many had been abused for years by church leaders and workers and felt bitter towards the Church. Many of them objected to holding the meeting in my church.

There'll always be times for them when things are bitter; there'll be the times when things are better too. You have to trust through the dark times. Ecclesiastes tells us that there is indeed a time for everything. In trying to find a way into the future, what's really important is loving compassion, and the loving compassion, which these people so clearly feel, will stay, but everything else might change. If they can trust and keep moving forward, they will draw strength from whatever was behind that Voice that spoke to me. It said don't worry; it said it'll be all right – everything might feel terrible at times, but it'll be okay as well.

*

Not everything is doom and gloom. To quote Gilbert and Sullivan, some things in my life and the calendar of Ashfield are a 'source of innocent merriment', like our Christmas Day lunch.

Christmas Day has a special magic for many of us – there is a sense of love that surrounds the day. Families come together. People fly in from all over the country to catch up. There are meals, celebrations and presents, but imagine if you didn't have any of that. Imagine if you faced Christmas alone.

My Kings Cross experience taught me that for many people Christmas Day is a nightmare, and so I decided to make sure that every Christmas I was at Ashfield we would have a free Christmas lunch for lonely and needy people.

The first Christmas, two people turned up and shared a plate of sandwiches. The next year thirteen people arrived and the next year fifteen. By then we had established the Loaves & Fishes Free Restaurant, so our next Christmas witnessed 400 people turning up for a meal. Nowadays, it's thousands.

Over 300 volunteers make that day special, and often their lives are changed by the experience. I always remember that I began as a volunteer and I still consider myself to be one. I do sometimes wonder where all the volunteers and the many members of my congregation come from. I've decided it's too difficult to work out and simply regard them as being sent by God.

I always feel that our big Christmas Day lunch with the homeless and needy is a spiritual event. It profoundly moves me. Last year I sat with a lonely woman who was separated and missing her children. In spite of this, she helped a distressed single mum calm her kids. Each woman found in the other exactly what she was looking for and was grateful.

That's what makes our Christmas Day so special. People reaching out beyond themselves. Strangers treating one another with loving compassion. It's the kind of thing that lifts my heart.

The lonely come and find a family they never knew they had. Perfect strangers become friends. Volunteers bring disabled people. Homeless people who have such low self-esteem they never go near crowds find themselves queuing with others for Christmas treats. Our big Christmas Day lunch is a truly holy event. For a little while people can put aside their cares and share in the love that was meant for us all.

*

On Christmas Day 2004, around 2000 people turned up for our free Christmas lunch. As usual, gifts and toys were flooding in so that even though we were giving toys away, by the end of the day we had more food and toys than we had begun with.

I was staring at the pile of leftover toys, wondering what to do with them that year. I had just returned from a trip to Zimbabwe and South Africa, so I thought I'd put aside any toys that didn't need a battery and send them there. However, the next day, Boxing Day, the earthquake off the coast of

It means so much to me to host hundreds of people every year at the Christmas Day lunch at Ashfield.

Indonesia caused a huge tsunami that devastated South-East Asia. I decided to reroute the toys to Thailand.

That night a woman rang a Sydney radio station and said that she knitted trauma teddies and wanted to send them to the darling little children in Thailand who had lost their parents to the tsunami. I told her to send them to me and I would send them along with the toys. Her story got out, however, and trauma teddy bears fell out of the sky. Millions of them! It got on the radio and the whole city of Perth took up a collection as well as Westpac and other corporates. Luckily the three-storey car park next to us in Ashfield was closed over Christmas: we filled all three storeys with teddies.

In order to get them to Thailand we had to count each teddy bear, value it, box it, and then value the boxes. You wouldn't believe it, but out of the blue someone from Ernst & Young rang and said their bean counters didn't have much work on over the next few weeks and needed something to do. They agreed to help value the teddies. Their eyes widened when they saw the piles and piles of teddies but they did the whole deed in a couple of weeks.

Other gifts arrived too: 750 kilograms of them.

At that stage we were actively sending much-needed goods overseas, an operation that was being overseen by my son Michael. To cut a long, long story short, we became great friends with Ilya Smirnoff and Khunying of Childline Thailand and Klaus of Poseidon CrusAiders. When Michael and I got to Thailand, people were still shaken up, mourning and grieving. It was really sobering being there and seeing the devastation that had been caused. I vividly remember seeing a ship that had been swept miles inland by the tsunami.

One thing I noticed was how so many international agencies gave the local people what they thought they should have, rather than what they needed. Instead of giving them wooden boats, for instance, they were giving fibreglass boats, which the locals couldn't repair. It reminded us how important it is to always ask people what they need, and to never assume you know what's best for them.

Over the years, and many trips to Thailand, I worked with Ilya and Khunying as they established The Hub, a homeless children's outreach centre situated right next to Bangkok railway station. Bangkok railway station is a hive of activity, as you can imagine, with runaway children arriving there from all over South-East Asia.

I have spent many hours on the station working with Ilya and the homeless children there. One of the children etched in my brain is a young Thai boy called 'Beer'. Beer was unusual in that he never lied and he never stole. He lived life as earnestly as he could. However, Beer had contracted HIV and life was difficult for him.

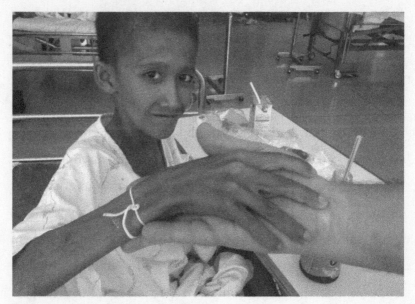

Beer, my young friend in Bangkok.

Beer and I used to talk a lot. He would take his anti-retrovirals when he was ill but forget to take them when he was well, so he would get ill again and then end up in hospital.

The last time I saw him he was so ill; he was in hospital, curled in a tiny shrivelled ball and crying for his mother. He obviously did not have long to live and I asked Ilya to let me know when the end was near. I told him I would be on the first plane over. Sometime later, when the phone rang and I saw that it was Ilya, I thought he was going to tell me that Beer was about to die, so I said, 'I'll be on the plane right away.'

'Don't come, Bill,' Ilya said. 'It's too late. His body has already been burned and buried.' In all the trauma they hadn't had the time to ring me.

Ilya told me about the funeral. In the Buddhist tradition you give merit when you die. Beer knew he was dying and asked someone to give him a twenty baht note to give merit. One of the Buddhist nuns told Ilya that Beer died clutching the note; he held it so tightly, they couldn't get the note out of his hand and had to burn his body with it still in his hand. Ilya told me, 'He died clutching his goodness, Bill.'

*

Some time ago I went to see a documentary called *The Apology*. It was about three Korean former 'comfort women' who were among the girls and young women kidnapped and forced into sexual slavery by the Imperial Japanese Army during World War II. The film affected me deeply.

I'd been following the story of the comfort women's fight for recognition and justice, as I really hate it when people have their truth denied. First one Korean woman came out and told her story and then others joined in, then Filipina women started and it became obvious there was a huge swathe of women who'd been grabbed and made sexual slaves of Japanese soldiers and officials.

I was in England when I read that Strathfield council in Sydney, which has a big Korean community, was refusing, under pressure from the Japanese government, to put up a statue in memory of these women. I was outraged and decided the statue could be erected in the grounds of my church, just a few suburbs away, if it couldn't find a suitable home elsewhere. Unfortunately, the Korean Church in Sydney was too scared to get involved so we held a meeting in our church hall with a lot of Korean people and between us agreed to erect the statue in Ashfield. The Koreans told me a lot of stories about the comfort women, and one particular tale of a Dutch-Australian woman then living in Adelaide – Jan Ruff O'Herne – really struck a chord.

Jeanne Alida 'Jan' Ruff O'Herne AO was a Dutch nurse during World War II. She was forced into sexual slavery by the Imperial Japanese Army in the Dutch East Indies (now Indonesia), where she was born. I flew to Adelaide to meet her. She was then in her late nineties, but we had a long talk. Jan had spent the previous twenty years campaigning against rape in war. She had suffered, but had reached a point in her life where she'd forgiven her captors and abusers. She brought me to tears. She told me how for years she had hidden her past from her husband, Tom. She was scared he'd reject her, but when she finally told him he loved her nonetheless for the strong, compassionate woman she was.

The Korean Comfort Women statue is in the grounds of Ashfield Uniting Church.

Speaking with Jan buoyed me with commitment and I swung into action; I started 'doing'. The statue was brought over from Korea, we had a celebration and the statue was installed. Then all hell broke loose.

The stories were everywhere: in the paper, on TV, online, on the radio. The Japanese Consul-General came to see me, and people from the Japanese Church, to tell me I was seeding division and had made the streets unsafe for the Japanese. They insisted that the comfort women weren't innocent victims but prostitutes. We had a lot of to-ing and fro-ing, and then threats were made.

One Japanese guy tried to rough me up. Then the New South Wales Minister for Multiculturalism rang and tried some gentle persuasion. Meanwhile, the Japanese community lodged a complaint with the Human Rights Commission, declaring that 'this hurtful, historical symbol is detrimental to the local community and will only result in generating offence and racial hate.' I got hauled before the Uniting Church administration. I dug my heels in and refused to remove the statue. This went on and on and on. But the statue still stands in the grounds of the church today.

A couple of years back, the Koreans invited me to a conference dedicated to the comfort women in Seoul. Three of the surviving women were there. One was Chinese, one was Korean and one was Filipina. All were in their late nineties and told their stories with honesty and dignity. What had happened to them was even worse than I'd imagined. If they were pregnant, they were forced to have abortions. One of the women had a baby that was killed, and after the war, when she went home, her own family didn't want her. The father of another of the women tried to kill her because of the shame. The Americans used the women when they drove the Japanese out, keeping the brothels going. These women had no one to stand up for them. They didn't just live with the horror of sexual slavery, but with rejection by their families and society afterwards.

We now have Koreans coming here to Ashfield from all around the world. They stand in front of the statue and cry. Some Japanese who understand what happened have started coming too; there was a group recently of mainly younger people and an older mother, and the mother couldn't believe what really happened – she couldn't believe Japanese people would behave that way. Anyway, the statue's there, it's not going anywhere and people make pilgrimage.

No one's made real reparation to the comfort women. There have been bits and pieces, but the issue got lost in the craziness of the Cold War and the separation of the two Koreas. The one thing that unites South and North Korea, though, is the comfort women. There's a network of suffering that bonds people even when politics divides them.

*

We have a Tiananmen Square statue too, commemorating the fourth of June protests of 1989 in which thousands of students died in Beijing. When Prime Minister Bob Hawke said all the Chinese students in Australia could stay, our church was one of the places where they registered for asylum. One of the students showed me a video of the students in Beijing building a papier-mâché Goddess of Democracy.

The Goddess of Democracy statue, Ashfield.

We have annual meetings here on the fourth of June and people come in memory of the slaughtered students. Since seeing the video clip, I'd always wished we had our own statue too, a Goddess of Democracy, even more so after I witnessed the democracy protests in Hong Kong in 2014. I was on the streets with the Yellow Umbrella movement, which demanded the right for the territory to pick its own leaders. It was basically run by students and gave me an idea of what Tiananmen Square must have been like. Before the violent official crackdown, I'd walk down Nathan Road, a commercial centre of Hong Kong, and there'd be study areas so that schoolkids could do their homework, and there were lectures on democracy. John Lennon's 'Imagine' was playing everywhere and quotes by Henry Thoreau and various American presidents were pasted up on the walls.

Back home, I had statues on my mind when, as if by a miracle, one of the local Chinese democracy people approached me with the offer of a statue of the Goddess of Democracy! The sculptor, Mr Chen Weiming of Hangzhou, China, had made three and this one had been a gift to the people of Australia, where he had lived temporarily. We placed it – a young female holding a torch aloft – in the church grounds. The ten-metre papier-mâché original, constructed in Tiananmen Square, was destroyed by soldiers, but our bronzed fibreglass version – like so many that have sprung up around the world since that fateful day – is a small but powerful symbol.

For many years I have been involved in pro-democracy and liberation movements around the world. That is because in the act of self-liberation you become aware of those living in chains. Among others these include people in Myanmar, the Uighur people in China, the Sudanese, and the Kurdish people. At one Kurdish meeting I made a heartfelt speech in which I said a prayer for the people of Kurdistan. I am proud to say the Kurdish people turned it into a song and it is sung throughout the Middle East. Who said events in a country like Australia cannot have a wider impact?

*

From my earliest days at the Wayside Chapel I became intimately involved in the lives of Australian Aboriginal people. This was because the Chapel had become a centre of Aboriginal activism. I continued on this course at Ashfield. One Sunday morning an Aboriginal woman called Aunty Shirley turned up for our church service and said she didn't really know why she came. 'Christianity is really a white man's religion,' she said, 'but I felt I had to come.' She talked about her son who has a disability. From that day, week after week, one of our elders would go with her to visit him.

Several Sundays later she got up in church again. 'I want you all to pray for me,' she said, 'because I'm telling my story to the Stolen Generations Inquiry tomorrow and I need your prayers.' We all prayed for her and gave her some flowers. A day or so afterwards, a photograph of Shirley clutching our flowers appeared on the front page of the *Sydney Morning Herald.* She had told the inquiry her story of being taken from her family as a child and how it had affected her and her family.

The next Sunday was Communion Sunday, and Shirley turned up with some friends. It was clear that the act of telling her story had disturbed her. Throughout the whole church service she couldn't stop talking to her concerned friends. She just sat in church and talked. When it came to communion, she still didn't stop talking. She walked up to the communion table and knelt, still talking away to herself and anyone else who would listen. I gave her the bread and she took it. I handed her the wine and, as she drank it, a moan came out of her that was soul-rattling. It was long and loud and painful. I stopped what I was doing, put down the elements of the communion, reached out and hugged her across the communion rail. For what seemed an eternity we held on to each other.

That day we all caught just a glimpse of how it felt to be Indigenous, taken from your family and alienated from your land. It was a really sobering experience. That Sunday is the only Sunday I know where the whole congregation went straight home after the service. Nobody stayed for a cup of tea or a chat. Everyone went home to mourn in their own way.

After that day, our work with Aboriginal people doubled, and Shirley is still with us to this day. She was one of the two Aboriginal women credited with stopping the riots the night Redfern burned, in 2004, following the death of Indigenous teenager TJ Hickey.

*

People find their way to us because – as I've already said – we're the end of the line; there's no one left to turn to. I know it's got something to do with the experience I had when Bob died. It's also got something to do with the fact that I don't give up; it's got something to do with who I am. It's got something to do with the idea that if you step out into the sunlight, something comes and meets you; the universe comes to you.

There are some things I don't get caught up in because other people do them better, but I often still support them. But no one's approached me with a cause I know I am capable of taking on where I've said no, I can't do that. I listen with my soul, and if it says yes then I do it.

RULE #7

**The twelve-step program is a good way to live.
Honestly, fearlessly examining your life.**

In 2014, I was contacted by a lady, Jessica, who had come across a film she wanted to show in Sydney, but couldn't get anyone to show it. It was an American film about people who were in long-term recovery from drug and alcohol addiction. They were speaking openly in the hope it would encourage those in the despair of addiction to keep trying to find a way out. They were living proof that it was possible. 'Of course, we'll show the film,' I said, and eventually an evening was set for the viewing. That evening was another turning point in my life.

We set up my Loaves & Fishes Free Restaurant that evening like a function centre. A meal was served and then the film, *The Anonymous People*, was shown. Well over one hundred former addicts showed up. At the conclusion, person after person told their story. Jessica got the ball rolling. 'I can now say,' she said, a quick smile flashing across her face as her hand touched her chest, 'that I am a person in recovery.'

Then Les Banton got up to talk. 'I was such an addict, even the criminals would have nothing to do with me,' he said. One woman talked of her shock at how far she'd fallen when she found herself in a public toilet shooting up with public toilet water. To look at that woman at the screening was to see a completely different person. A young man got up and said, 'The jails are full of us addicts. We need to talk about our recovery, that recovery is possible, and I am so proud to be in this room.'

The honesty was breathtaking and had a powerful effect on me. I realised that sharing your innermost secrets changes them into a story and liberates you from their power over you. It's a good way to live, I thought, and vowed to attempt it myself.

Ever since that day I have regularly met with Jessica, Les and others in recovery. It has changed my life so much for the better. I try now to live a life devoid of those secrets that can so debilitate you. Of course you can't divulge everything to everyone, but you can find individuals to share appropriately with so your secret becomes a story and its power over you is removed.

Out of those meetings has come the Sydney Recovery movement. Every year we hold a Recovery march to which hundreds turn up. The march goes from Circular Quay up Macquarie Street, past Parliament House where we give

The Sydney Recovery walk – an inspiring annual event.

speeches, to the Sydney Domain. In 2015 the New South Wales premier, Mike Baird, walked with us. To an onlooker suffering drug or alcohol abuse the message we aim to give is one of hope. 'If all these people can do it, then maybe I can, too.'

So much of what has happened to me in recent years, particularly my improving relationship with my children and my opening up to others so that I am no longer the perennial outsider but feel part of various communities, has come about because of my discovery of the Recovery movement. Although in many ways the movement is aimed at people battling to overcome drug and alcohol addiction so they can lead meaningful lives, it also helps individuals overcome loneliness and alienation to become the person they were truly meant to be.

Australian social researcher Hugh Mackay has said that one of the things people regret most at the end of their lives is not having been honest with each other when they had the chance. So cut out the bullshit. Look into someone's eyes and think about what you really want to say to them. It's hard because all your barriers will come up. But once you say it, the barriers come down.

CHAPTER EIGHT

REAL TROUBLES

In the 1970s Ted Noffs was charged with heresy and I saw first-hand the profound effect it had on him. He was deeply, deeply troubled by it. He could talk of practically nothing else and he and his barrister, Jack Hiatt QC, spent countless hours discussing strategy and writing letters. Ted was eventually cleared by the Methodist Church of this charge but the scars remained. Years later a Church bureaucrat said to me, 'We would never have found him guilty, Bill.' I thought of the blood, sweat, tears and anguish that the charge had caused and couldn't help but think to myself, why then go through the farce of the trial? I may be wrong, but I truly believe that it contributed hugely to Ted's eventual stroke and early death.

Everyone agrees Ted was a difficult character; I believed if I behaved differently towards the Church authorities I wouldn't end up in a troubled relationship with them. I should have known better.

When I first arrived at Ashfield we had no money. We did not even have enough money to buy postage stamps. The minister's office had been cleaned out and all that remained was a telephone answering machine that didn't work. So I rang the bureaucracy to ask if they could give me the money for an answering machine. Their response was, 'Oh, Bill, you can raise that money yourself.'

Of course I could and did. But I realised that in trying to do anything at Ashfield I was on my own.

Over the years I have had my trials and tribulations with Church bureaucrats. I quickly learned that whether it is Ted Noffs or me, the institution doesn't like those who stick out. When I first started taking in homeless children and the stories began entering the media, an inquiry was held into what I was doing. I simply kept soldiering on. That was when I really began to feel on the outside.

At another stage I was working with someone and I knew I had to get them to leave. There were rumblings that we could be involved in a racism charge, which everybody knew was not true, and I had to endure the indignity of going through the process of having my, and my congregation's, integrity questioned. During that time, I went to mediation with this person and every week I said, 'I will not work with you.' Every week I went in and said the same thing and the Church's response was to put my church into caretaker mode (which my congregation did not appreciate) and strip me of my ministry while they did their investigation. Just like for Ted Noffs, the allegations were found to be baseless and I resumed my ministry.

At one time a major company was giving the Exodus Foundation, in today's money, about a million dollars towards building a new facility. I had filled in the required Church forms only to find out a bureaucrat had contacted the company and asked them to put the money towards a different Church activity, rather than giving it to Exodus. The company executive, with a mystified look on his face, said to me, 'Who would do that? That's not a very ethical way of operating, Bill.'

The global financial crisis (GFC) was another bad time for me. Our literacy program involved a hundred schools in the Sydney area and several in Darwin. We had our overseas work as well as the Loaves & Fishes Free Restaurant, and we were doing well under the banner of the Exodus Foundation. Everything was operating as I had imagined and hoped for when I first came here. Then the GFC hit and we were in a really tight place moneywise. I could have borrowed money from a local bank who had agreed to loan it to me but Church officials said, 'Borrow the money from us, Bill.'

Regretfully I did. In making the loan the Church took control of the Exodus Board. Programs I had invested my very soul in were in line to be sliced off and closed down.

In order to keep these programs operating I quickly established the Bill Crews Charitable Trust. And as these doomed Exodus projects were closed down by the Exodus Board on a Friday evening, I reopened them on Monday under the Bill Crews Charitable Trust. Money came in to the trust to keep them operating.

At that time Church bureaucrats were pushing me to retire and said they would honour my legacy. But my fear was that upon my retirement, they would close everything down.

My suspicions were confirmed a few years later when one person in the Synod (the Church council) told me that as soon as I left, everything would be closed down. As I relayed this to staff members, they said to me, 'Bill, these programs are so important and so much good is being done, we must keep them going.'

I should have realised this because way back in the 1970s, when I was exposing the plight of runaway children and failed adoptions, the Methodist Church pressured Ted to shut me up. To my undying gratitude and utmost respect, Ted told them where to go. One little Aboriginal girl who I would come across in Kings Cross kept running away from a state-run institution and once said to me, 'I would rub my

Each day, hundreds of people come to eat at the Loaves & Fishes
Free Restaurant. (© David Barnes)

dark skin against the bricks hoping the colour would rub out
so I wouldn't be raped so often.'

In the past I have sought the help of the Uniting Church
with difficult situations and with funding programs, and I
have found to my dismay that I cannot rely on the institution.
In fact, most times I have found that the institution's response
to me and my work has been heartbreaking. In spite of all of
this, it is the good people in the Church who I am grateful for.
Every person I have worked with has their heart in the right
place. Congregation members, ministers and bureaucrats
donate individually but as an entity the Uniting Church
does not. I find this a real conundrum. How it is that I have

received so much help and support from individuals within the very bureaucracy that has made life so hard for me?

A few years ago, there was a minister, John, appointed by a Church committee to investigate all the programs I was running. He wrote a really positive report. He continued to provide report after report every year until he retired. Even then, he kept making personal donations towards my work. As he got older he could only send twenty bucks. And he would send it over and over. There are people like that all through the Church who just get it and support me and my programs out of goodness and love.

After I placed the statue of the Korean Comfort Woman in our church grounds as a memorial, I was hauled in for a grilling. But I stood my ground, not blinking, and they ended up supporting me.

One of my great friends, and fellow travellers, is Father Chris Riley, the CEO of Youth Off the Streets. Chris is a Catholic priest of the Salesian Order and he told me an instructive story not so long ago: the world head of the Salesian Order was in Australia and a local dignitary was showing him around; they drove past Father Chris Riley's place but they didn't go in. The Salesian Order was at the centre of sexual abuse cases in Sydney in the 1980s and Father Chris was overseeing the operation of twenty-five programs with 200 staff and 400 volunteers aimed at helping young people deal with that history of trauma and abuse. But the head of the order wouldn't deign to visit one of their own who's worked hard to counteract the damage done by the Church.

Jesus wept all right.

*

Life is an enigma. We will never make sense of it. Life is what just happens. It is what we are born into and struggle with. Our brains try to make sense of what is basically senseless.

The worst times are when you feel truly alone. When you feel nothing is working and you are at the bottom of the pit. It doesn't matter if your friends and loved ones try to help you; the situation you are in leaves you truly on your own. You look around and it seems as if no one is there. You feel like you're sitting in the enormous emptiness of life.

Yet I have found those times to be times of profound learning. Times when, from the very bottom of the barrel, we pull above ourselves and learn from the experience. So rather than fearing those times we should embrace them.

One of the important things I've learned is to actually *live* in the enigma called life. To sit in each unique situation and deal with each situation as if it has never happened before.

Conditioned responses deny the feelings that each unique situation presents. We have to be alive in the moment.

There is only now. The past is over and the future is yet to be. If change is to come for us human beings, that change must begin now. I have learned that I cannot change you, you cannot change me. The only power I have is the power to change myself. The only being I can change in the whole of existence is me.

Change must begin with me, now.

RULE #8

Practise the difference between empathy and sympathy.

Empathy is when I say to you, 'Gee, you're having a bad time'; sympathy is when I say, 'I feel so sad and sorry for you having such a bad time.' With sympathy, you're injecting yourself into someone else's issue; with empathy you're understanding the issue. Sympathy is paralysing; empathy can open you up. I've found that a lot. Somebody who's dying will ring me up and I'll want to say, 'I feel so sad' or 'I'm so sorry', but it's much better if I say something like 'You're facing the inevitable, aren't you,' as then I can help in a practical way.

This is a hard rule, and the better you get at it the harder it gets! You realise how much of yourself is caught up in other people's problems, particularly if they're people you really care about and you want a certain outcome for them. It's like the story of Jesus and the rich young man, whom Jesus obviously cared about. The rich young man asked Jesus what he had to do to gain eternal life, and Jesus told him to give all possessions to the poor and follow Him. The young man walked away and you can feel the terrible pain in that story for the young man, and Jesus's love for him. Jesus listened to the young man and gave him the best advice; He didn't wring His hands and tell him how sorry He was for him. So, it's hard if you love someone and they're in pain and you know what they should do, but they're not going to do it.

There's a book called *Never Split the Difference: Negotiating as if your life depended on it* by Chris Voss, who was the lead international kidnapping negotiator for the FBI. His work brought him up close with hostage-takers, bank robbers and terrorists and he learned that you have to get inside their heads and mirror back to them what they are. You get them to tell you their situation and the more they tell you, the more they begin to trust you and the more you can begin to get a solution.

I don't work for the FBI or ASIO, but on a daily basis – on air or on the streets – I talk to people in the worst of circumstances. I tell them what I see, I don't interpret what I see; I ask them to tell me. It's subtle, but it works. Often when I've practised empathy and avoided sympathy, magical things have happened.

One morning Sally, a young Aboriginal girl, turned up as usual for her literacy program. Sally had obviously had a bad night. Her young face was dark and thunderous. The teacher came up to her and said, 'You look like you've had a tough night, Sally.' Sally threw up her arms and shouted, 'Fuck you. Fuck your school and fuck the whole world.' Nobody needed to say anything else; they knew exactly what she was feeling.

CHAPTER NINE

THE AFGHANI BOY AND OTHER MIRACLES

My experiences of the Voice that I've already described are not the only spiritual experiences I've had. There have been many other occasions in my life where something has come to me, often to move me forward when I've found myself stuck. I have absolutely no idea why this happens to me. It just does. I know the experiences are true and I can believe the Voice because of the caveat that came with the initial calling: 'And by the way, your personal life won't be that happy.' That bit, that's the caveat.

Consequently, I've come to understand that with every gift there comes a cost. I often compare the experience I've had to that undergone by singer-songwriter Yusuf Islam, aka Cat Stevens. For Yusuf, the cost of his 'Voice' – his religious conversion, his faith – was that he didn't play a guitar or use his wonderful singing voice for forty years. It seems to me that the cost attached to any calling, however great or small, is what makes the experience real and valid. The personal cost to me has been the loss of not one but two marriages, which brought pain to my ex-wives, to my four children and to me. I now realise how difficult life is for those who are very close to me. And though I'm working on opening myself more to others, this has created a loneliness which I just have to live with.

Because if there's ever a choice between the mission and whatever else might be calling for my attention, the mission will win. Though I do try to clearly ascertain where I'm more needed. And even though the people closest to me should be aware of that, it can still hurt.

One year there was a drama going on that demanded my presence and attention at the same time that I was meant to be celebrating my birthday with the family. They had a birthday party for me, with a teddy bear in my chair. I didn't have the emotional maturity then to deal with the family hurt.

One of the benefits of this stage of life I am in now is being able to see my children as adults. All children embrace their adult self when they are ready. And I am so proud that all of my children are being the best adults they can be. Now as a father and a grandfather, I really value the loving relationships I have with all my children.

Being a pastor to the lost, hurt and needy is my vocation. I've tried to explain that over and over to others, but sometimes it just doesn't sink in.

I have also realised that any power, success or prestige I've acquired doesn't rest in me, but in my staying true to that Voice. I'm just an ordinary, wounded, weak human being and I struggle sometimes to do what the Voice requires, because what the Voice requires often isn't easy. So I try to follow Jesus's words: 'Don't be afraid.' As someone wise said, 'Fear is a bad advisor.' Time after time in staying true to the Voice, I have had to put my personal fear aside. This is not easy, but I find that after the event I always wonder why I'd been afraid.

Living on the edge can be difficult and painful and not where everybody (particularly Church bureaucrats) wants to be. So although society on the whole likes what I do, I am a source of anxiety to Church bureaucrats. Consequently, my personal relationship with those who try to keep the Church in good order is edgy. I know that's an outcome of my being true to the Voice and that's as it should be. If my relationship with the bureaucrats was an easy one, it would be because I fitted in with their business plans and wasn't doing my best for those in need. The Voice told me to work with those who don't fit into any business model, so that very edginess is a necessity.

*

Mahboba's Promise is a not-for-profit organisation dedicated to helping women and orphaned children in Afghanistan. A Muslim woman, Mahboba Rawi, was a fourteen-year-old student activist in Afghanistan when she was forced to flee from Soviet soldiers occupying her country. With her family she travelled through the Khyber Pass and across Pakistan as a refugee. She and her family were eventually given asylum in Australia. Tragically, her new homeland would be the setting for disaster. Mahboba and her extended family were having a picnic at the Kiama Blowhole on the south coast of New South Wales. They were standing at the edge of the blowhole when the water rose up with unexpected force and washed them into the hole. Her son drowned along with six other family members and friends. Mahboba was devastated and went into a deep depression, which from time to time returns to dog her to this day. She realised the only way forward was to help others, so she set up schools for both kids and women in Afghanistan and raises money to run them via the charity Mahboba's Promise.

One day Mahboba was showing me photos of the kids at school in Afghanistan and pointed out a little boy called Seir. He had a huge curvature of the spine, and Mahboba told me that when he hit puberty he would die, because his bones would harden and squash his lungs, killing him. Seir was twelve then and everyone was really worried about him. The clock was running down mercilessly on this boy's life.

I rang Bob Woods, our Exodus doctor, who, like many other professionals, has given his services, free, to Exodus and the Bill Crews Trust for many years. I explained Seir's spinal condition as best I could. Bob had a mate knowledgeable in the field and undertook to ring him.

The mate couldn't do anything, but recommended a surgeon he believed could fix Seir's spine. The surgeon was operating in Ashfield at the hospital just down the road, right at that moment! I told him the story, showed him Mahboba's photos and he said he'd need some special rods, but he could fix Seir's problems. There was a bonus: the surgeon, Dr Angus Gray, said he'd operate for nothing.

Following Dr Gray's advice, I rang Rotary Oceania Medical Aid for Children (ROMAC); it's the branch of Rotary International that brings kids from developing countries to Australia for operations. They usually only bring children from the Pacific region, but are allowed one case outside the region each year. That spot was free, and Seir could have it. ROMAC organised the hospital – the Prince of Wales in Randwick – so all I had to do was get Seir to Sydney from Afghanistan, at that time a very unstable, volatile country.

I'm good mates with Brendan Nelson, who at that time was the Commonwealth Minister for Defence. I rang Brendan and trotted out what was by then becoming a well-worn story. He listened and then he said they'd throw him in the back of a plane. There was an RAAF Globemaster supporting the Australian defence forces in Afghanistan which did 'mail runs' to Sydney once or twice a week. Brendan referred me to Brigadier Someone-or-other, who I would have to go and see in person, in Canberra. He would be the one taking care of the logistics.

I went down to Canberra and fronted up at the brigadier's office. He listened, looked at me and said, we're not going to do that: every time the military tries to do something good it becomes a disaster; we end up with egg on our faces. There had recently been a stuff-up regarding the repatriation of deceased personnel from Afghanistan, and according to the brigadier it had demoralised everyone. I said, 'But the Minister of Defence said—', which was all I could get out, because he looked at me with steely eyes and said, 'I don't give a fuck what the minister said. I won't do it.'

I felt like I had a guest role in an episode of the satirical political sitcom *Yes Minister*. I went to see Brendan and the look on his face was a mixture of incredulity and resignation; it was clear that he ran up against the likes of that brigadier all the time. 'What are we going to do, Brendan?' I asked. 'We've got this little boy, he's got to have an operation.'

Things happened. Did they ever. Within a day, two business class return airfare tickets from Afghanistan materialised, courtesy of the Department of Foreign Affairs and Trade (DFAT). Brendan had rung Alexander Downer, the Minister for Foreign Affairs, and got the tickets out of the DFAT budget somehow. I'm not sure if any of this made it across Prime Minister John Howard's desk, or whether my guest role in Commonwealth affairs was elevated from *Yes Minister* to *Yes Prime Minister*, but that's how those two tickets came to be.

Seir's uncle travelled with him and the Afghani community here stepped up to welcome and care for them. We got down to business as quickly as possible as that health clock of Seir's was ticking away. To complicate matters it was discovered he had tuberculosis in his bones as well as the curvature problem. The doctors had to first of all fix the TB. That meant Seir and his uncle had to stay here for a good while, and we organised for Seir to go to school. He was good at soccer, which was great for his morale, but the doctors were freaking out because of his chalky bones. Seir got through that unscathed, the doctors got rid of the TB, and the day of the operation loomed. By then several months had passed and Seir was starting to feel the very real effects of his hardening bones; we were getting dangerously close to our window of life-saving opportunity closing.

Dr Gray, the surgeon, not only prepped Seir for surgery, he prepared me too. He told me that it would be a fourteen-hour operation and Seir could die. When they wheeled that young boy into the operating theatre, I didn't know whether I or anyone else would ever see him alive again. I lit every candle in the church I could find.

Then I rang Shirley Maddox, a former New South Wales Moderator of the Uniting Church and a wonderful woman. I'd met her at theological college, where she became one of my mentors, and we have a friendship to this day.

I said, 'Shirley, he's just gone in. He can't die after all this, after all the miracles that brought him here; how could God allow him to die in the operation?' And she said, 'Bill, if Seir dies, God will be with us in the grieving.' And BANG, I understood, it all became clear to me. God wasn't sitting upon his high whatever weighing up the pros and cons of whether this little Afghani boy would or should survive the critical operation. That was now in the hands of the good Dr Angus Gray and his skilful team. But God was in there with them, God was with me and God would be there whatever the outcome.

I was still in the church, fourteen hours later, holding vigil among the candles, when I got the phone call from Dr Gray. It was all I could do to fumble the buttons and take the call. Dr Gray was crying and through his tears he said, 'You know, Bill, we had to get these steel rods into his back, special iridium rods which Johnson & Johnson donated to us, and we did that, we put the poles in and then we waited.' He told me that all the machines went silent. The team waited and then, he said, all the lights came on and it was like a Christmas tree. 'It worked,' he said, 'and he'll be okay.' Dr Gray and I were both bawling our eyes out. Seir stayed here for a long time recovering before he returned home, and he now manages a quarry in Afghanistan.

It all could have so easily gone the other way. I know and understand science; it might not have been that all the lights came back on. But God would still have been a compassionate presence: in the operating theatre, in the church where I was waiting, in Seir's home village where his family was waiting for the news, in the homes of the Afghani community in Sydney. That's what Shirley was talking about and that's the God we're all looking for.

*

In 1999, I was awarded an Order of Australia and marked the occasion with my brother-in-law Peter, my eldest son Michael, my sister Ann and my mother Barbara.

Over the past forty years there have been temptations for me to move away from my initial vision. As I've noted, people like to tell me that not all our Loaves & Fishes guests are 'battlers', and suggest that arrivals be vetted so only those in need receive a free meal. My answer is that often the poorest of the poor have little self-confidence and would feel intimidated by having to prove their credentials, not to say humiliated, and might thereby go hungry. One of my favourite sayings is: 'We need to kiss a lot of frogs to kiss a prince.'

I also need to confront the temptation to move our work from helping the poorest of the poor to those who are 'easier' to work with. Working with the poorest children from the poorest schools can certainly be difficult and there are 'better behaved children' who could certainly benefit from our programs. My answer is to say that if we're not experiencing difficulties with difficult kids and people then we are not doing our job. Sometimes other people think I'll have some magic solution to their problems, and clamour for my attention, hoping to turn it towards them and away from our programs. And in my personal life the temptation has often been to forget about work and go and live in a shack on the beach.

I know, though, that if I don't keep true to my visions and the Voice, and instead give in to the tempters, then the miracles, the donations and the rescue money will cease to flow.

Over and over again Exodus and the Bill Crews Trust have been saved by a donation appearing just in time. In February 2011, for instance, we were again in a severe financial crisis. We had emptied every hollow log we could and were $499,587 down on our $500,000 overdraft from the bank. Our situation was dire. Out of the blue the phone rang. It was a lawyer in Melbourne telling me he had an anonymous donation of $900,000 for us and asking which account he should put it into. It was as if that call came directly from God.

Then, in 2012, I was a pretty sick man. I was overweight and I knew my knees would have to be replaced. My self-esteem and confidence had shrunk away to nothing due to arguments I was having with individuals in the Uniting Church Synod who questioned my work with the poorest and most needy people in this world. It was around this time that I established the Bill Crews Charitable Trust.

I felt that those goodly Church bureaucrats were quite happy for me to be like Ronald McDonald, the smiling happy clown who brings in the money. It was okay for me to be the face of the Exodus Foundation, but they considered themselves the arbiters of where and how monies raised should be spent. They did not like some of the work I was involved in and the people I was working with, especially my projects overseas or anywhere really outside Ashfield. I was saddened by their narrow-mindedness and judgemental attitudes and the fact that all the work I'd done over the years meant nothing to them. The encounters were bruising, character assassinating, brutal and soul destroying.

That's not all there is to tell about that story. In January 2012 I went to hospital for my double knee replacement. The operation was complicated and I had to stay in hospital longer than anticipated. It had been arranged that after the operation I would be transferred to a particular rehabilitation hospital to recuperate. However, the extended length of my stay in hospital meant I had to do my rehabilitation elsewhere.

As luck would have it, I ended up in a rehab hospital close to Ashfield, and became quite close to the head nurse, who had to regularly arrange my dressings and drips and all the rest of it. One evening, at the end of his shift, the head nurse and I were talking. 'By the way, did you get that $900,000?' he asked casually as he inspected my tubes. My blood went cold; how did he know about the life-saving $900,000 donation of a year previously?

He told me the story. The previous year the rehab hospital had experienced severe financial difficulties and had to put off staff. One of the hospital workers affected was a cleaner called George. His hours were severely reduced and his wife, who also worked at the hospital, was made redundant. They were in dire straits. Receiving his last full pay cheque, George went with his wife to do the shopping. After buying groceries and other necessities they had six dollars left. George said to his missus, 'Do we buy a cup of coffee or a lottery ticket with our last few dollars?' She said, 'Let's buy a lottery ticket.'

That ticket won them tens of millions of dollars. George was intellectually challenged, as were his children, so he found a financial advisor who bought properties for George and his wife and the children and invested the rest. Because George had reading difficulties, he knew the value of reading.

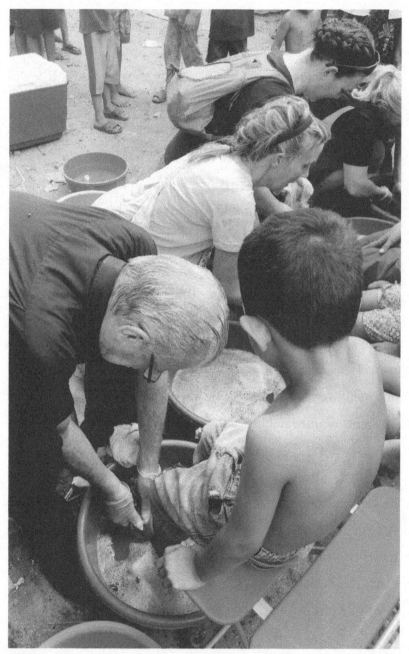
Washing the feet of children in Poipet, Cambodia.

There was still plenty of money and he told his financial advisor he wanted to give $900,000 to me, as he knew about our literacy programs, and the same to Father Chris Riley of Youth Off the Streets. What a selfless, compassionate soul!

Out of that came the phone call. I checked the dates and they all added up so I know it's true. What amazes me is that it was purely by chance that I ended up in that rehab hospital and purely by chance that I befriended the head nurse. It was a miracle upon a miracle that I learned of George's story, and that he made the donation. I am truly humbled to this day.

Still in the rehab hospital, things weren't going too well for me medically, despite the wonderful attention and care of the staff. I experienced a sense of helplessness I never want to feel again. It was an old nurse who eventually got me up and walking. 'I can't do it. It's too hard,' I moaned. 'Come on, we'll do it together,' she said, and I slowly began the long process of walking my way to recovery.

Shortly afterwards, Dr Bob, our Exodus doctor, told me he wanted to make sure I was fit and healthy. So for the next year or so I went through every medical test available. I even had my brain looked at. I found a dietician and lost over thirty kilos. I found a sports physiotherapist who gave me a set of exercises to do to keep me healthy for the rest of my life. Every day now, to keep fit, I walk for forty minutes and do the exercises prescribed for me.

So I emerged victorious bodily, but my self-esteem remained badly damaged and almost destroyed. It was on the rubbish tips of Cambodia that my long slow spiritual and emotional healing process began. There, I met Andrea and Malena who worked with kids who'd been abandoned by their families and trafficked for sex. Seeing Andrea and Malena work with those children with such love and affection and witnessing them doing things that I'd been pilloried for, and feeling all those feelings I'd been ridiculed for, reaffirmed my commitment to helping those in greatest need and helped ease my broken spirit.

There are miracles that happen in my life that baffle me.

One involved our work with ex-prisoners in Australia. I've had a lot to do with them over the years and appreciate the problems they face once they've done their time. Les Banton visits jails and we get letters from people in jail who are about to be released and are worried about what they'll do when they get turfed out. Because all they get upon release are the clothes they went in with and a garbage bag of belongings, plus two weeks' pension. That's all. Which means that often they find themselves out on the street in prison greens with a garbage bag and nowhere to go. Not surprisingly, they can turn back to crime and land back in jail and the cycle goes on.

I wanted to help set up a system to look after these people. I met with Michael Coutts-Trotter, who's now the Secretary of the New South Wales Department of Communities and Justice (so he's the CEO of the prisons) to see what I could do. In 1986, Michael received a nine-year prison sentence for dealing heroin, so he knows about both the difficulties of restarting life after prison and offering a message of hope. The program we developed is slowly evolving and will support ex-prisoners both before and after they leave jail.

Meanwhile, I received an email from a new graduate of the Uniting Church's theological college, who wanted to know if I had any vacancies at Ashfield. I didn't have a vacancy, but we met for a cuppa and I asked her what her dream was. To my surprise and delight she said, 'To be a prison chaplain.'

Something similar happened with our literacy program. For years we ran it through a company called MultiLit, which ultimately wanted to move in another direction. We'd put more than 3000 kids through the program in Sydney, Darwin, Gladstone in Queensland, and lots of other far-flung places. We had to close down much of what we were doing, but we kept going in Darwin.

For two or three years I searched for another literacy program because I knew how great they were for kids. I wasn't having any success until I had a long overdue catch-up with one of our wonderful donors, Jane Mundy. We were finally sitting down together and she asked me how the literacy programs were going. I explained about MultiLit and how their pulling out made my blood boil. Jane smiled and said, 'Bill, my best friend who lives in England has spent years putting together a literacy program called Everyone Can Read. She's just come to Australia because her daughter's getting married here in Sydney.' I secretly suspected that Everyone Can Read would be another white elephant of a program, but I got my staff to check it out. They came back and said quite the opposite, that it was really great. I rang Suzanne Attwool, Jane's friend, and the day before she returned to England we met and got our program. Miracle! These things happen to me all the time, and I can't explain them – but I am endlessly grateful for them.

There are so many other miracles I can talk about. A man heard me on the radio once for five minutes between flights. He sent me a cheque and told me not to bother finding him as he was only in Australia briefly. I did find him. His name is David Boehm and he lives in Hong Kong. We became friends and he and I now work together on programs in Thailand, Myanmar, Cambodia and Hong Kong. As I've already mentioned, my work there began after the tsunami in 2004 when I was fortunate enough to meet Ilya and Khunying at Childline Thailand, and this continues to this day. In 2008 Cyclone Nagis devastated Myanmar. We sent a forty-foot shipping container loaded up with aid, which was the only Australian aid the generals allowed in. And my son Michael and Tim Costello were the only Australians the generals would allow in.

*

Forty years ago, I could not have written about my spiritual experiences. I would have been too shy and embarrassed. Now I'm proud of them. I know they are not manifestations of madness or simply the way my brain copes with pressure. There have been too many outside influences and happenstances for this to be something happening in my brain alone. Something outside must be involved. Too many people have rung at the last minute with rescue money for my work; too many times someone has appeared out of the blue with the very thing I need to continue my programs. Yet I can't become complacent or smug. I am always grateful. I have been given a gift and it's my solemn duty to use it to the best of my ability to benefit those I feel I am 'told' by the Voice to help.

RULE #9

Don't be afraid of the truth. It will set you free.

Whenever the homeless kids who lived here at Ashfield Church were arrested, I'd go and sit with them while they were questioned by the police. The kids would answer as truthfully as they could; you'd get the lot – true, real, honest. I remember thinking, I wish I could do that; I wish I could be like that, with no filter. Did you steal that? the police would ask. Yeah, the kid would say. Why'd you steal it? Because he did this, so I stole that. What did you do over there? I did this and that, so what? They didn't hold anything back.

Finally, I did let the truth set me free. It was when I talked about both my marriages. When I was able to see them as stories. When I didn't try to hide anything. I wasn't withholding part of myself and so could engage with others more openly and genuinely.

To be with people when they are at rock bottom or not travelling well, that's a holy place, I think. It's when a lot of truth comes out. I experienced it recently when a woman, who many people had described as being difficult, spoke out.

She's part of Milk Crate Theatre, a therapy theatre group we set up. In one of the workshops, the participants had to write something and read it out. This women got up and said, 'I don't like churches much, don't like religion much, it's bullshit. But when I sit in the Loaves and Fishes and have a meal there, that is my holy communion.'

Holy communion is not just a sacrament of the Church. It happens every day in normal life.

*

I've gone to the sordid and the squalid places in this world because God's there. I relate my experiences not to save others, to save you, from doing that; I'm not bringing back the gold from those places to give you so that you can vicariously experience getting that gold. No, I'm saying go there. I'm saying go and look for yourself.

I'm encouraging you to go and see that truth – wherever it is – for yourself. The truth is not so scary. If you go there, your life will be changed – as mine was when I went to the Cross – and don't be afraid of that. I'm not going there and bringing it back, I'm saying come with me. But people rarely come. Human beings are conservative by nature, so people don't do anything or change unless they have to. Nobody gets into a twelve-step program unless they've hit rock bottom.

Nobody skips joyfully into the rooms of AA, NA, GA or any of the other Anonymous groups saying how glad they are to be there. They're lucky if they crawl in on their hands and knees, saved from the hospital, the psych ward, the morgue. I've heard the gratitude, seen the restoration to sanity, seen the help they give to their fellow sufferers. I've seen the alchemy of base lead turned into gold, seen the pariahs and outcasts of society turned into those who are of use and make this world of ours a better place.

If I could send people to a place to have a look, I'd say go where the Australian women married the ISIS soldiers. They sometimes took their children with them to lives of terrible hardship and horror. I played what part I could in bringing the orphaned Sharrouf children back to Australia. The oldest girl, Zaynab, had been married off by her ISIS fighter father to another ISIS soldier at the age of just thirteen, and had given birth to three children by the time she was eighteen. I hadn't been involved with them at all, but then a wealthy businessman rang me and said he wanted to give them money – because their Australian grandmother, Karen Nettleton, was looking for money to bring them back from a refugee detention camp in Syria – but he didn't want anyone to know who he was; he wasn't looking for fame, he just wanted to help others. He gave me $10,000 cash in a brown paper bag to give to Karen. I hadn't met her before but gave her the money and she went to Syria with an ABC TV crew, but the transaction didn't work and she needed more money; it was demanded of her. I went back to the businessman and we had this monstrous fight: he said, why should I give you, a gormless preacher, any more fucking money? I gave back as good as I got. I liked him, but I stuck to my guns and told him Karen really needed another $5000. He was worried that the money would end up with ISIS (and yes, you have to pay bribes to get children out of ISIS), but a grandmother's love for those abused kids was more important. In the end he gave it to me.

And in the end Karen didn't have to pay ISIS. I had even met with a former SAS operative based in England who brings kids out from places like that. However, Karen got them home herself.

That's where God is. That's where some uncomfortable truths are to be found: refugees are people just like us who've landed in terrible circumstances through no fault of their own. In acknowledging this truth we can set ourselves free from the distortions and lies too many leaders try to foist upon us. A grandmother's love is the truth.

CHAPTER TEN

RADIO TIMES

In 2002 I received an invitation to host a radio show on 2GB. The station had been broadcasting since 1926 and was originally owned and operated by the Theosophical Society, an organisation with interests in humanity, religion, philosophy, science and nature. There had always been a Sunday night religious program. Fred Nile, the conservative Christian minister and politician ran it for a long time, and when he left he was replaced by Gordon Moyes, another conservative minister and politician, who, like Nile, was ferociously anti-gay.

Moyes, who'd been the superintendent of the Wesley Mission, went so far as to say on air that many biblically faithful Uniting Church congregations would no longer want to belong to the Church if it passed a resolution to ordain practising homosexuals. He condemned on air a female Uniting Church minister who was in a relationship with another woman, and suddenly there was all hell to pay as millions of dollars in defamation and privacy lawsuits flew around.

John Singleton, who was a big stakeholder in the station at the time, rang me up and asked me to go on air and calm the waters. It was 'trouble in Ashfield' all over again, only this time the problems were on the airwaves. I thought I'd be replacing Moyes for maybe two or three weeks so I agreed. In those first shows I had to read a prepared statement every half hour apologising for what Moyes had said. That was in 2002. Unexpectedly, the program ratings started to go up and it just went from there. I am still broadcasting every Sunday night nineteen years later.

Now the show has the largest Sunday night listening audience in the history of Australian radio. Four times the number of people listen to me as there are Uniting Church members. I am continually amazed by the number of listeners who contact me and say they don't go to a traditional church anymore and regard my radio program as their church service. I think of the show as a secular talkback program run by a minister, embracing everything from current political debate to 'Will you say a prayer for me because my loved one has died'. I play music that is not religious and try to engender a sense of awe around the wonder of life and how we need loving communities to enable life to flourish and grow. Perhaps I've taken the idea of that cherished song book from my Wayside days – *Travelling to Freedom* – and made it a living thing on the airwaves.

I learned the craft of live broadcasting with Brian Carlton (now at Triple M, Hobart) as my senior producer for my first ten weeks or so on air. He'd hold signs up with instructions for me: stop here, finish here, say this or say that. He taught me patiently and kindly, and since those early days I've been teamed with Jason Kerr. As so often happens with people working with me, the job expands to become more than a job, it becomes something real, so Jason will often tell me that he doesn't want to produce anybody else after doing this show. It's a much-treasured partnership.

I love radio, even though I'm a little constrained in what I can say and what music I can play because I know the limits of the audience and I've learned not to be self-indulgent. I only play tested popular music. I'd like to play Dylan, Tom Petty and some other music that might not be well known or appreciated by the show's listenership, but I also want to look after my demographic so instead I'll play Elton John. Maybe I'm wrong, but I understand that I have to toe some lines in order to push other boundaries. My dear old gals at Ashfield would let me do whatever I wanted in church as

On the airwaves on Sunday nights.

long as I didn't fiddle with the hymns. *Quid pro quo*. Even so, I try and push the agenda.

In the beginning it was a real shock to me to come across so many people more conservative in their thinking than I am, more in tune with my predecessors on the program and other big names on the station. I'd tended to think of those famous names like Alan Jones and John Laws as unique; however, their listeners all tend to think like them and they're out there in their millions. Being on the radio really reinforced to me there are plenty of people who have different points of view. I've had to learn how to push the boundaries and yet make sure that they still listen, because they're not my natural congregation. I've had to choose my battles. For instance, I don't talk a lot about the plight of refugees *per se*, but I might talk about Omar who's lost his kid and his leg. I'm not shying away from the truths of our world that I believe in and hold dear. I'll give listeners the world as it is and also let them come to the program with their thoughts on any given topic of the day.

I hosted the show for about the first seven years for nothing, no payment. Then Singo wangled it so I got paid as a casual presenter. I wasn't interested in the money, I was more interested in the show as a missional vehicle: not necessarily promoting Jesus, just sharing and exchanging compassionate thoughts with listeners, with the broader community.

*

One Sunday night I was rung by an older gent who had stopped playing tennis a few years earlier, because he couldn't see the ball clearly. He went to the optometrist who fitted his specs with a new prescription and when he tried tennis again he saw two balls. He said to the optometrist, can't you make it three and they'll all coalesce into one? You can see why people like him live so long; they don't know how old they are and they've got an optimistic attitude to life, always looking for the humour and fun in situations. At the end of the call he said, 'I want to tell you a joke, Bill.' He said, 'I'm at the shopping centre with my trolley and I lose my wife and as I go looking for her I bump into another guy with a shopping trolley, a bit younger than me. I say to him, "What are you doing?" And he says, "I'm looking for my wife." I said, "So am I." I said, "What does your wife look like?" and he said, "She's twenty-seven, she's busty and she's wearing shorts." I said, "Oh, I'll help you look for yours."' The caller telling me this story was ninety-two years old.

Then there was a woman, eighty-five, who had married an accountant and all he cared about was money. To quote her, 'He was a miserable bastard.' She belonged to a lot of church groups and was involved in many charitable activities. She was really sad because her husband had taken her to task for spending thirty-two dollars on their son's Christmas present; she told me she didn't know what she'd do without the support of her church groups. I asked her if her husband helped out with the charities. He told her he'd done enough for the church. She was trapped with this 'miserable old sod', but hadn't let on to her children how mean he was. I said a prayer for her and told her to keep doing her church work because it was keeping her sane.

Though every caller is unique and has their own story – maybe of heartache, maybe of good humour – those two calls are typical of the show. I try to give every caller my focused attention and have them end the conversation feeling that someone has really listened to them and affirmed their humanity.

*

I did an interview with Father Bob Maguire, the Catholic priest who's made it his mission to provide material, emotional and social support to whoever needs it, and who used to host a radio show on 3AW in Melbourne. We talked about what we thought should be on the agenda for us, as a community, to look at. Kindness, we decided, should be on the agenda. More and more people are finding themselves isolated and affected by the unkindness of society. We'd both noticed this from talking to callers on our respective shows over the years. I think it's because people, as individuals, are finding life harder and consequently becoming less kind and more intolerant. That's exacerbated by the fact that across the globe there's no inspiring leadership, or very little. Too many of our leaders just dissolve into the chaos of politics, compromising themselves to stay in power, rather than planning for the future with compassion and care.

Some politicians have impressed me. I was with (ex-prime minister) Kevin Rudd a day or so after he was rolled and he said, 'It's like I've dropped off the agenda, nobody's sent me messages.' I told him he'd done so much good, and in a tiny voice he said, 'What do you mean?' Well, I was lucky enough to be in the House of Representatives at Parliament House in Canberra on 13 February 2008 when he issued the formal apology to Indigenous Australians for the forced removals of Australian Indigenous children, the Stolen Generations. I said, 'Look at the good you did in that.' He did that, and through the GFC he held the country together.

From the other side of politics I also get on really well with Philip Ruddock, who's had two terms as a minister in government, and Brendan Nelson, as I've already mentioned.

When my son Tim was six, I noticed that a little boy around the same age would sit on a bicycle in the church driveway, just watching. He'd be there every afternoon. After a while I managed to talk to him and we got really friendly. His mum was dead and he and his dad lived in a block of flats just opposite the church. His family was from Africa and his dad was pretty much a womaniser who used to spend a lot of his time at a party house, leaving the little kid all alone. He wasn't looked after very well, so Gill and I took him in and he and Tim used to sleep one each end of Tim's bed, top to tail.

As time went on he became quite a favourite with the old gals and other members of the congregation. One day the dad came to me and said, 'I'm being deported, can you help me?' He'd overstayed his visa. We'd been getting counselling for the little boy and his psychiatrist told me that if the boy was shifted again it would do serious damage to his mental health. The old gals weren't going to let that happen. Even though they believed themselves to be 'non-political', they hosted Liberal Party meetings and would flutter around like headless chooks whenever Bronwyn Bishop or other party luminaries turned up. They came to me and said, Bill, you go down to Canberra and see Philip Ruddock – who was then the Minister for Immigration and Multicultural Affairs – and tell him that if this little boy gets deported we will lie on the tarmac at Sydney Airport and the plane will have to run over our bodies. I duly went down to Canberra and got an appointment – because I think Ruddock knew about the old gals who hosted Liberal Party meetings. He looked at me as if he knew already what was going to happen. I don't know what took place but the boy and his dad stayed.

*

A woman rang the show as we were talking about influential people in our lives. She spoke about her father, one of twelve siblings, whom she loved more than anything. Then she began talking about her husband and the story got dark. They had a son and a daughter who'd both run into problems, and it turned out the husband had sexually molested both of them when they were little. The listener told me this one-to-one, yet there were nearly 200,000 people listening. People ring in and tell me the most intimate things in their lives as if it's just them and me talking; they've got no one else to share it with. They're isolated, sometimes in the midst of a crowd of family and acquaintances, and that can be dangerous for people.

A 96-year-old man rang in, truly sounding in desperate straits. It turned out he couldn't get an erection anymore and didn't think life was worth living. I said, don't worry about your erection, mate, you're lucky to have lasted to ninety-six! More seriously, I tried to connect with him by listening to him and acknowledging the deeper hurt and loneliness that lay behind his tragicomic confession.

This is what I try to do: help in whatever way I can. I try to let people know I'm ready to hear about their experiences, whatever they may be. I want them to know that I 'get' them and will sit with them in their pain, their worry, their joy.

A psychiatrist I know of who takes on the really hard cases that no one else can fix took on a particular woman who was chronically depressed. Nobody before had been able to help her, but he did and her depression lifted. She told the psychiatrist that for the first time ever she felt that somebody 'felt me'.

If people feel 'felt', they move towards goodness and compassion, and that's what I try to achieve whether from behind a microphone or a pulpit or out and about in the world. I try to metaphorically (and often literally) sit beside people, so they can feel they're not alone in the deepest part of their soul. I think if you get in there and do that – and often it's a scary place to go – people start to feel they can change. That allows people to heal themselves. As somebody once said, it's not rocket science. But it's hard work. If you can get in there, truly, with someone in their pain, they heal themselves, and they feel they're not alone. I think that's what Jesus did and urged His followers to do.

*

In late 2013, John Singleton commissioned filmmaker Warwick Moss to produce a documentary about our Christmas Day lunch. It was a collection of vignettes and stories of the poor, needy and lonely, and the volunteers who turned up to our free Christmas Day lunch celebration. As the filming progressed, Warwick and I became firm friends and realised we had the makings of a really good documentary team.

Immediately afterwards we began work on a TV and online series called *Stories from the Edge*. We have since made almost eighty half-hour episodes, which detail the lives and stories of many of the characters I come across in daily life and the effects they have had on me.

These are stories of people who permanently live life on the edge, the often invisible people who we walk past without noticing. And if we stopped to listen to them, we would hear an amazing story.

As the series went on we realised it wasn't just the poor, homeless and needy who lived life on the edge. Many of us live lives like that. So our storylines expanded. As you can imagine, many people who we have profiled and interviewed have since died and so our stories have become a living testament to them.

Stories from the Edge has become a catalogue of how life can throw really bad stuff at you which is so hard to overcome. Our filmmaking has morphed into many shorter YouTube videos expounding on this theme. Now, every week, we also film a ten-minute church service.

Many times, for us, the act of filming becomes an event in itself. At one stage we were threateningly moved on by a security guard as we attempted to film outside a large residential property.

Along with my 2GB program, this has given me a real opportunity to share what I do, and the people I meet, with a wide audience. To date our YouTube series has had well over 1.5 million views.

The stories continue to this day. What began as a helpful act from John Singleton has produced all this.

*

After the Lindt Café hostage siege in Martin Place in 2014 when Katrina Dawson and Tori Johnson were killed, I was rung by a family friend. The Anglican Church wouldn't bury 34-year-old Tori Johnson, the café manager who was posthumously awarded the Star of Courage, because he was gay. I said of course I would. I met Tori's mum and dad and family and the funeral took place at St Stephen's Uniting Church on Macquarie Street in Sydney, just a few seconds walk from where the siege had occurred. The family laid a wreath in Martin Place before the service; it was a field of flowers and people coming to add tributes talked of being able to smell the fragrance long before they reached the site, such was the volume of floral arrangements placed there.

Not a month later, in January 2015, I was in Paris when the Île-de-France attacks happened, including the shootings at the offices of *Charlie Hebdo*, the satirical weekly newspaper. I walked to the offices in the 11th arrondissement and laid some flowers. Sometime later in Sydney, all the flowers that had been laid in Martin Place were about to be composted, so I asked the New South Wales premier, Mike Baird, if I could take some of the compost to sprinkle at the memorial that was planned for the Charlie Hebdo victims in Paris. At first he said no, not wanting to link cities in terrorism. But he must have had a change of heart because later, on Christmas Eve, a plastic bag full of composted flowers turned up at Ashfield for me to take to France, as I'd be leaving on Boxing Day for my annual visit. By then the Bataclan Theatre bombing and other attacks had also taken place in Paris. I was due to meet some officials there as well.

I wondered how I was going to get the bag – which looked like it was full of hash – through customs. I was flying via America and England and could foresee all sorts of problems. So once again I rang Brendan Nelson. His former private secretary was then the head of customs and she advised me to post the compost, labelling it 'church supplies'. I posted it on Christmas Day and off it went.

Miraculously, both the compost and I arrived in London, and I went over to Paris on the Eurostar for the Charlie Hebdo memorial service at the Place de la République. President François Hollande led the commemoration, many thousands of Parisians attended and the French Elvis – Johnny Hallyday – sang on a bitterly cold day in January. It was moving, touching and inspiring.

As part of the ceremony, a ten-metre-tall oak tree was planted. Long after the service was over and the crowd had dispersed, I quietly went and mixed some of the compost in the soil at the base of that tree, so there's a bit of Australia there. I met with the staff and performers of the Bataclan Theatre before returning to London with the remainder of the compost. I didn't know what to do with it, so there's a big bag of composted flowers in the ceiling of the monastery in London where I stay, waiting for me to return and find meaningful fertile soil to add it to, which I will. I will also go and see how that oak tree in Paris is growing in its own fertile soil, enriched with the love and compassion of so many Australians.

RULE #10

**Realise life is not a self-focused thing;
realise we are all part of each other.**

It's an in and out thing, isn't it? As I've already said, what goes on out there in the world affects you inside, which affects the way you interact with the world. There's constant feedback. Often we are different with different people – and this is a concept that scientific research is now examining and confirming. So it makes sense that the core of us is less individualistic than we'd like to think. There is no diamond at the centre of me or you or any of us. We're influenced by what goes on around us and in the wider world; there's no one set of rules that can tell us how to behave and think. We're not individuated economic units as some politicians and economists would have it, and extreme individuality just creates neurosis. I hear it on the radio when people ring in, in their echoing, anguished loneliness.

Many People of the Book, whether they're Christians or Muslims or Jews, want to rip out their soul and put their particular Book in its place – the Bible, Koran, Talmud, take your pick – which reduces life to a series of laws. Those barriers that people put up when they wave their Books around get in the way of everything.

I've had enough of putting people in a box and I think it's damaging. One person's path can illuminate another's. I would say Jesus influences my life a lot, but some of what the Buddha did has influenced my life too. Buddhist people are as much a part of my journey as Christian people are, and so are Muslim people, Jewish people: life is life. I was with a rabbi the other day and he said, you're just a universalist, and I thought, well, that's a good thing.

I see too many religious leaders promoting conservative cultural dogma rather than religion. When it's the Dalai Lama's birthday, we change the church into a temple and the Tibetans come and perform their rituals and meditation, they put their garlands up, and to me this is the definition of a true place of worship: that a place can be both a church and a temple; it's just a holy building where we all come together. People expect me to be tolerant and respectful, to promote interfaith gatherings and concepts, but sometimes they don't expect that I'll be changed by doing that. The truth is, for me, that if you're human, you're vulnerable and everything can change.

Marcus Borg was a widely known American New Testament scholar and theologian of the most progressive type. He acknowledged that though he came from a really heavily biblical tradition, there were two people who had most influenced him in the world: one was Jesus, the other was Buddha. He strongly believed that a meaningful and faithful Christianity in the twenty-first century should not discount inquiry into and influence by other faiths.

Matthew Fox, another American, was formerly a Catholic priest. He is a follower of Thomas Merton and really into Creation Spirituality, which emphasises a holy relationship between humanity and nature. The Catholic Church chucked him out when he questioned extremely conservative Christian tradition and he joined the Episcopal Church, working with young people to reinvent forms of worship. He's brought dance, DJ-ing, VJ-ing and more into the Western liturgy. His Cosmic Mass, rooted in Judeo-Christian tradition, is supported by leading-edge science, and bears witness for social, environmental and gender justice. It has been celebrated in dozens of cities in North America.

Ted Noffs too was a person who didn't limit his theological searching and influences. He started as an evangelical Christian, but threw the restrictions of that strand of Christianity away because he realised that in real life, in Kings Cross, it didn't work. He used evangelism in a modern way, and to see that was inspiring. He showed me that people are looking for spirituality without barriers; we're all in the messiness of life together, everyone's looking with hope in the same direction, searching for goodness and compassion. We're all travelling in our different ways, via our different faiths, to get there; we're all heading to the same destination, just choosing alternative routes on the map.

*

There's a film clip you can watch online of a boy asking a question of Pope Francis. It's just beautiful. The Pope visited a parish on the outskirts of Rome and invited the younger parishioners to come to the microphone and ask questions. One boy, Emanuele, was overwhelmed, and no matter how hard he tried or was coaxed he couldn't ask his question, so the Pope invited him forward to whisper the question in his ear. He then asked Emanuele's permission to tell the audience what his question was.

It turned out that Emanuele's father had died a short time earlier. He had been a non-believer, but had ensured his four children were baptised nonetheless. Emanuele wanted to know whether his dad, who had been a good man, was in heaven.

That boy deserved a caring answer, not just something intellectual. He'd asked a big question, but he was also talking about the hurt he felt. The image of that little boy clinging to the Pope is hard to watch. The Pope answered the question in a theological way, but then he hugged Emanuele, trying to heal his hurt. Being told that your father is in heaven is okay, but there's more to it than that, isn't there? He got a wonderful acknowledgement of how he was feeling with that hug.

What troubles me though was that the Pope was surrounded by a bevy of cardinals who were probably ready to knife him if he stepped one inch outside the party line that they're boxed in with.

Emanuele was already affected by the judgement of some in this world that his father couldn't be in heaven because he didn't go to church. Even at the age of six or seven he'd already got the message that if you're not a believer, it won't bode well for you on the other side, no matter what you do on this Earth. No wonder he'd looked so worried. Hopefully the Pope's answer and actions reassured him that it's not whether you go to church or not, it's how loving you are while you're here that's most important.

The question remains though: how do we overcome the barriers some people erect around religion, barriers that aim to divide the world into the worthy and the unworthy? (I sometimes think that if it's all about the Book, whichever Book that might be, aren't we worshipping the teapot and not the tea?)

Well, over the years, as I've already said more than once, I've learned the enormous power of just sitting with people: not judging, just being a loving presence. We simply need to acknowledge that we're all part of each other. 'Each man's death diminishes me,' wrote John Donne when he was Dean of St Paul's in London in 1624. It was as pertinent then as it is today. 'Therefore, send not to know for whom the bell tolls, it tolls for thee.'

Many's the time I think it doesn't matter how we 'get there' – whether it's via Judaism, Islam, Hinduism, Christianity or Buddhism. (I really hate giving religion a name; to me it's all one spiritual quest.) The important thing is to be on the journey. Jesus talked about this all the time. Remember the Good Samaritan who wasn't a Jew or a Christian? And the priest who walked on by because to touch a sick man would make him unclean? Those sorts of rubbishy rules and distinctions are what give religion a bad name.

There's another story in the Bible where Jesus healed a blind man on a Saturday. The Pharisees went for him because he worked on the Sabbath; how could he be a religious man, they said, when he worked on the Sabbath? It's so much better to focus on the good in religion, in people, and live with loving compassion. At the height of the first wave of coronavirus in Italy a 72-year-old Roman Catholic priest was on a ventilator in a hospital bed and a young man in the bed next to him wasn't. The old priest told the nursing staff to take the ventilator off him and give it to the young man. They did and the priest died. He was true to the real meaning of religion to the end.

*

There's an associate professor, Amit Bernstein, from the clinical psychology program at Haifa University in Israel who's been teaching mindfulness to asylum seekers. These people who've fled horrifying situations and conditions have learned to live with their loss and trauma with Bernstein's help, because the outside world doesn't determine what's inside a person, what's inside these marginalised refugees. Rules and objective 'certainties' can't define us.

When Mother Teresa's diaries were published after she died, they revealed all her doubts about the existence and nature of God, leading many to declare there can't be a God if even Mother Teresa had doubts. But the open-minded theologians of the world said that that's what we struggle with all the time. Our thoughts and feelings grow and change, and only the most hidebound believe we should unthinkingly and unchangingly adhere to a certain set of rules that our heads and hearts need to question.

That's why it was so important for all of us that little Emanuele asked *that* question of the holder of one of the highest religious offices in the world. The Pope took the opportunity to send a message of compassion, not dogma. There's intellectual certainty, and there are emotional, compassionate responses – and the two conflict at times.

I heard of a brain surgeon in the UK, a man of great faith, Jewish. He said that outside of the operating theatre he relies on his faith, but once in the room, scalpel in hand, it's about science; he still has his faith, however. The two don't have to be exclusive. Nothing has to be exclusive. You bring it all into the room, you bring the whole panoply of life into the room.

CHAPTER ELEVEN

EXODUS AND
TRAVELS

Today, the Exodus Foundation and the Bill Crews Charitable
Trust are separate arms of the Rev Bill Crews Foundation.
We've been rebuilding ever since the Church tried to shut us
down, and all our programs are now in a period of expansion.
We thought a lot about how we could move forward and be
most effective and we've gone mobile, so that now our food
vans are giving out as many meals as the Loaves & Fishes
Free Restaurant, which is running as strong as ever.

At the moment we have two vans: we go to
Woolloomooloo, near the Cross in inner Sydney, and we
go to several sites near Liverpool, in south-west Sydney.
But we're expanding our reach and I hope that we'll have

six or seven vans before too long. We'll target the lowest socioeconomic areas of Sydney.

And good people have promised us a million dollars, which means we can put dentists and doctors into vans and even get them into remote communities, though there's also a lot of need in Sydney. Every winter, I used to bury far too many homeless people who'd died of pneumonia, so we started giving everyone who came to Ashfield a free flu shot and the funerals dried up. It's often as simple as that. We carry out blood pressure tests too and screen for hepatitis C, and are looking into the problem of people not being able to afford prescription medicines. As with our food vans, we want to send our medical vans to the lowest socioeconomic areas where they're most needed, and make them satellites of what we do here at Ashfield.

We're also building our literacy program back up, and will soon have six schools across Australia. Already we've graduated something like ninety kids. We target the areas to go to by looking at the NAPLAN results and other socioeconomic indicators.

In all I've done I've concentrated on those who have no one. The outsiders. The almost 1200 meals we provide each day are directed towards those who are homeless, needy or lonely. Our literacy tutorial centres focus on the poorest kids from the poorest families from the poorest schools, aiming to

The Exodus food van feeds hundreds of people in Sydney each night.

People's lives are reflected in their feet. When I wash someone's feet, I find it a spiritual and moving experience. It's also a connection with Jesus and what he did.

break the cycle of poverty and prevent the kids from hitting the streets.

But there are lots of other things we do which are more traditionally church-related. For me the most moving is our yearly 'washing of the feet' of our guests in the Loaves & Fishes Free Restaurant. This takes place on Maundy Thursday, the Thursday before Good Friday. Together with volunteers I wash the feet of the guests who turn up that day for a free lunch. 'Do you wear your robes?' a Church elder once asked me. The whole event is actually too holy for that. Stripping back the pomp and ceremony of religion and focusing on the meaning of Jesus's teaching (or Mohammed's or Buddha's) is the way to go, I reckon.

Exodus is a special place and I feel really fortunate to have seen it grow. It's wonderful to have been part of creating a space where one deprived person can show another where to find food, education, respite and comfort. Really, isn't that what life's all about?

*

A project I'm working on now is aimed at getting chronically unemployed people into work around the new Sydney airport being built out past Liverpool. An 11,200-hectare Aerotropolis, a hub of technology, will also be built, as will a railway line from St Marys to the Aerotropolis. But we're not just dealing with the chronically unemployed, we're dealing with their families too, for if you're serious about moving people out of unemployment, you've got to work with their kids as well. If we get a group of adults back into the workforce, their kids will need to be minded: there's a child-minding issue to tackle as much as an unemployment problem.

We run a long day care centre in Summer Hill, so we've had experience already of working with young kids in trouble, and my time at both the Cross and Ashfield has given me a lot of exposure to older kids with problems. We plan to set up a trauma-informed centre for kids aged from under one to six years old at the Aerotropolis, which would also offer family therapy, a centre for kids aged six to twelve who are in danger of dropping out of school, and a similar space for teenagers. All of them would be disaffected kids, but if we help them they may end up with a job rather than continuing to shoulder the family curse of unemployment. What we're envisaging is a wholesale transition of people from poverty to work.

We want to do the same thing in Tower Hamlets in London, because the same issues are going on there. And that was where my father and his brother used to walk around picking up manure, just to survive, so that'll be my memorial to Dad.

*

The phrase 'bitten off more than you can chew' should perhaps resonate with me, but things happen and they have to be attended to. Life will have me heading north-west and suddenly I'm diverted east and then south and then wherever. I see it as giving people a chance in life; that's all the team and I are doing. We don't walk away from people in need because they don't fit into some carefully calibrated plan.

However, there's a lot about the Church – the Church that I'm a part of – that gets in the way, and almost seems to want to thwart me. There is no perfect institution anywhere, but if I was working for a business and I had great ideas that were being blocked, I'd move on to somewhere else. Sometimes I struggle to reconcile my relationship with this organ that is 'the Church'. With the advent of the Rev Bill Crews Foundation, I really don't need the Church anymore to do what I do. So why do I stay within the Uniting Church fold? I have to say that in spite of everything, I love it with all my heart. Its foundation document, The Basis of Union, excites me whenever I read it. All churches can trace their heritage back to the laying on of hands, to the earliest time of Jesus.

As years ago, in a different age, Ted Noffs's wife, Margaret, used to say, 'It's that bloody brotherhood. It gets them every time.'

*

A lot began to change for me when I found the Wayside Chapel and a community of people who felt as odd and alienated as I did. I realised I wasn't alone in the world; there were other people who felt like square pegs in round holes. I established many programs to help them and others like them while I was there. But even in establishing those programs I was always on the outside, the one looking in, the one forming groups for lonely people – but doing it for them, not for me. For many years night-time found me going home lonely. Even when I married and knew I was an integral part of the Wayside set-up, I always felt a little like a lost child observing a happy family through a pane of sound-proof, shatter-proof glass, longing to be part of what I could see, but not knowing how to break in.

Over the past ten years I have gone through the often-painful process of rebuilding my relationships with my family. I can honestly say now the sound-proof, shatter-proof glass is nowhere to be seen. In addition to that I have found an international family – a family trending in the same direction at the same time, just in different spots on the planet. I find I am now in a group – not part of the group. Not merely managing it from the outside. Not a day goes by without me being filled with tears, some joyous and some not. I feel like I have embraced and am embraced by a family. The relationships are deep and loving. With this loving comes pain and mourning. For I have found that the more we love the more we hurt. But it's worth it. It's worth it because with every tear I know I am alive; with every heartbreak I know I *feel*; with every love comes the sadness of parting.

Every time I go to London I stay at a monastery in Highgate with the Passionist Fathers, an order that was set up a hundred-odd years ago. My connection with them started with a priest called Ray Brain who used to volunteer at the Wayside. He was really good, we used to work together on the streets of the Cross and we became good mates. But when I left the Chapel for college we drifted out of touch. I didn't hear anything of him for years until I was in London and an ABC reporter, who was there to do a story about me, mentioned an Australian priest I might like to meet. It was Ray Brain! I couldn't believe it. Ray was living in the monastery at Highgate and I stayed that first time for two weeks. He and I walked all around London. Ray's back here now, in Adelaide, but the priest who took over from him is another Australian. I am looked after by, and feel part of, that wonderful community.

In Calais, at the Jungle, I also made a deep connection. I went up to the guy who'd organised the NA meeting that I was welcomed in to, and introduced myself. His name was

Alireza. He lived in Paris and came to Calais every week to run the meeting. In the oft-quoted words of Humphrey Bogart in the film *Casablanca*, it was the beginning of a beautiful friendship. (In my imaginary re-enactment Alireza plays the part of Claude Rains, while I keep Bogart's role for myself.)

Now every time I go to Paris, I see Alireza. He's Iranian and escaped from Iran with a friend whom he describes as having the face of an angel. They made it to Greece where they got into some heavy-duty business, both dealing drugs, including heroin. The angel-faced mate's brother came over from England to try to rescue him, but he died of an overdose. The brother did get Alireza out of Greece and out of trouble, and that's why Alireza drives the three hours from Paris every week to the Calais Jungle to hold NA meetings. 'His brother rescued me,' Alireza said, 'and I do NA in gratitude.'

Alireza and I wander the back lanes of Paris, meeting up with the local addicts. We sit and talk with them, and Alireza will point out venues where NA groups gather, trying to help without judging. One day we were talking about the St Francis Prayer, which is one of the favourites of the twelve-step movement, and is well known to a wide Christian audience too.

Lord, make me an instrument of your peace.
Where there is hatred, let me bring love.

Where there is offence, let me bring pardon.

Where there is discord, let me bring union.

Where there is error, let me bring truth.

Where there is doubt, let me bring faith.

Where there is despair, let me bring hope.

Where there is darkness, let me bring your light.

Where there is sadness, let me bring joy.

O Master, let me not seek as much

to be consoled as to console,

to be understood as to understand,

to be loved as to love,

for it is in giving that one receives,

it is in self-forgetting that one finds,

it is in pardoning that one is pardoned,

it is in dying that one is raised to eternal life.

Alireza knew the prayer by heart, but he didn't know who St Francis was. I told him to go to the Louvre to look at a twelfth-century sketch on wood of St Francis. I couldn't help but think there'd be something special in this work for my friend, as it depicts St Francis being visited by Christ in the form of a seraphim, an angelic being.

Alireza has his own opera group, and often performs in French theatre. He's done all right, but he hasn't got citizenship and he's just been cleared of hepatitis C. He's now a marriage celebrant and he is such a smooth operator that he's making a fortune, yet he can't get a French passport because of his days as a refugee addict on the coast of the Aegean. But he continues to give of himself to his new communities in Paris and Calais, and people come from all over the world to be married by him. Alireza's like a really close brother to me. A boy from England's Hertfordshire and a boy from Tehran. Who'd have thought?

Another great friend on the other side of the world is Anne Marie in Glasgow. Like Alireza, she's come out of addiction and dedicated her life to saving others. Anne Marie's whole family were alcoholics, but Anne Marie got sober and studied for her master's of social work. She now runs Recovery UK. Every year we hold a Recovery march to a UK village. Usually around 16,000 people turn up and it's a great celebration of people in recovery. I am proud to be an integral part of it.

When I first went to England, I looked for someone to help me publicise the Big Picture film festival. It took me a long time to find someone – and then I found Jenny Rose. We still work together and I am honoured to be officiating at her wedding.

Meeting Alireza, Anne Marie and Jenny, and others like them, brought me in from the cold, into the centre of life. My history of setting up communities but always being separate from them is now behind me. I've learned how shallow that was and how I need to be *part of* something. A lot of hugging now goes on around Exodus and in my life in general. Because of my newfound friends, I'm learning to be closer to my children and feel privileged to be gradually becoming a bigger part of their lives.

One day a woman called Bridget came to one of our film screenings. She pulled me aside after the film and said, I can see into your heart and I want to work with you. Her name is Bridget and she's a Black minister from the US. We worked together for a few years and it was with her that I learned about casual racism; I saw it through her eyes.

So my blood family, and others in Australia, together with Ray, Bridget, Jenny, Alireza, Anne Marie, Ilya in Thailand and Clare in Calais, you have made me a far better person with your loving acceptance and encouragement of me just as I am.

*

Along with my commitments in Australia, I try to spend time working overseas. My travels include a regular trip to the US. First I travel to New York, to a group called Urban Pathways that I work with. Their mission is to ensure that homeless and at-risk New Yorkers have the housing, services and support they need to be self-sufficient.

There's a social worker there who's a dead-ringer for a female, seventy-something Robert De Niro: she's got his face and hair and the same attitude. A typical New Yorker, she's seen it all, worked with kids in trouble, run refuges and women's shelters. We were talking one day and I happened to bring up the subject of adoption, saying that probably a third of adoptions fail. Suddenly she got really interested and told me her story.

She was from Italy and her parents couldn't look after her properly, so they sent her to an aunt in New York who adopted her, but she was abused really badly. As she spoke about being a kid, her face changed; it started to glow like a child's. It was moving to see that dyed-in-the-wool 'seen it all' New Yorker shed her armour to look at life in a childlike way again; that ability to empathise has stood her in good stead as she helps kids who are in trouble now.

From New York, I head south to Fort Myers, Florida, to see Bill White who is one of the leaders of the Recovery movement. He's not in the best of health now, so he can't travel very much and the medications he's on leave him really vulnerable to viruses, so I just go and sit with him. He's taught me how spirituality and recovery are intimately linked. The two hours I might spend with Bill are more than worth the long diversion to Florida.

When I fly these great distances, I usually just sit. In the beginning I used to take plenty to write or to read, but now I just sit and let whatever happens happen. I try to open myself to people, to experience and to learn.

From Florida I fly west to San Antonio, and catch up with my Texan 'family'. Years ago I was on ABC Radio's *Conversations* talking about adopted kids and as I left the studio, feeling really vulnerable, my phone pinged and it was a Facebook message from a fifteen-year-old girl, Samantha, in America, saying, 'Is it possible you might be my grandfather?' She went on to say that her maternal grandmother had been married to a Bill Crews in California in 1972, but he'd since disappeared out of their lives. I emailed back and said no, it's not me; I didn't set foot in America until 1978. But something she'd written really struck me – Every mother needs to know who her father is – because it echoed what so many adopted kids used to say to me: I need to know where I get my green (or brown or blue) eyes from. The next day was Father's Day here in Australia, so I sent her mother, Christina, an email, saying, 'Even though I'm not your father, Christina, I can understand how you're feeling.' That opened the floodgates and Christina sent me her life story, email by email. We corresponded over the next few months and eventually agreed to meet the next time I was in America.

I got to Chili's Diner just outside San Antonio and took a seat by the window, waiting. Christina and her three daughters drove round and round the diner, trying to get a peek at me, to make sure I wasn't a weirdo. They must have been satisfied by what they could see and eventually we all had a lovely time together.

We kept emailing after I returned to Australia, and the next year, when I returned to America, I spent a day with Christina and her family in San Antonio, and now that's an annual tradition. I guess I've become her surrogate father.

I just hang out with the family. We usually have breakfast together: Christina, her husband, Michael, the three girls and me. If Christina goes shopping I'll go shopping with her. What I really like is that they're a real family and they're all in it together. One of the daughters has had a baby and the baby's had lots of brain issues. The whole family looks after the baby, Michael too – there's none of the male sitting around not being involved attitude in that household.

Christina's is one of the few places where I can put my mind in neutral and just hang out for the day. I'm not the Reverend Bill Crews when I'm there. I'm just Bill. I recharge my batteries for the work that's always waiting for me back in Sydney and elsewhere, and I'm forever grateful to my San Antonio family for that. And I'm grateful for the way they unselfconsciously show me the way to try to connect more deeply and genuinely with my blood family, something that's important to me in the time left to me. I want my children to see and connect with the real me, not the public me.

*

Occasionally someone connected with my public life will ask how *I'm* going. One of our regular guests at Ashfield had really bad eyes and I raised the money for him to have an operation. He had been a misery, on massive amounts of medication, but after the operation he came to thank me for helping him get his sight back. He asked me how I was and I did something I rarely do: I told him how I really felt. I said, 'Mate, I've got a bad leg and I've got a headache and it's Monday and I'm exhausted because I did the radio program last night.' He looked at me and said, 'Ah, shit happens, doesn't it.' In a loving and laughing way I thought, thanks for nothing, mate. But he got the public me on track again with his down-to-earth response.

Sometimes I feel like a triangle of billiard balls on the green baize of a table just after the white ball has crashed into the arrangement, fragmenting it in all directions. Each of those scattered balls feels like a bit of me. I've been trying to gather those balls, those bits of me, back together for a long time. Just being 'Bill' when I travel helps with that.

I used to go and sit in the coffee shop in the atrium of the Westin Hotel in Sydney's Martin Place sometimes: it's noisy, impersonal and yet pleasant all at the same time. I could sit there and be alone with me. But one of the waitresses came up to me recently and said, 'What would you like, Mr Crews?' and I thought – even as I laughed to myself – oh, no, I've lost my anonymity.

Last year, a bureaucrat in the Uniting Church said to me, 'Bill, why don't you retire and do all the things you want to do? Then you would have all the freedom you want.' My answer was, 'Why should I make life easier for you?' I had been expecting that question for quite a while and had thought about it. What struck me was that even if I did retire from the Church, I would still do exactly what I do now.

After all this time I have a lot of expertise, experience and knowledge. My early work with kids running away from institutions, adoptive families and abusive situations has taught me how poor we are as human beings not only in looking after our own children, but other people's too. My work with drug and alcohol dependent people has taught me how Western society has taken to heart the belief that drugs and/or alcohol will make you feel better. My work with the homeless has taught me that society doesn't want to look after our wounded brothers and sisters.

My passion for the underdog has, if anything, increased over the years. I see how the 'born to rule set' – as the former prime minister Paul Keating contemptuously calls them –

actually believe they run the world and deserve to, and inflict unbelievable hardship on those who don't fit into their narrow vision of what life is all about. We're living in an increasingly divided world, pitching brother against brother, country against country, society against society, religion against religion, the rich against the poor, ignorance against science – and it's my feeling I can be a force for good in all of this.

It's taken me a lifetime to learn what I know now, and act on it. If you remember the song 'I Am a Rock' by Simon & Garfunkel, well, that was me in 1970, before I went to the Wayside Chapel. I was a rock, so I know what it's like to be on the outside, holding in my pain. I know what it's like to have nowhere to go to find comfort, to be soft. So what I'm trying to do is create an environment where people can be soft; it's not a weakness. Neither is it a valued commodity, but it should be. Being soft allows us to let go and share and to aim for a better world.

RULE #11

**You can only discover yourself in the company
of others. You can't do it alone. We learn who
we are by looking in the eyes of others.**

I believe that when we gaze into another's eyes, we vanish;
we tap into a pure consciousness that's very loving. I often go
walking with my Buddhist friend Ilya when I'm in Bangkok.
He talks Buddhist stuff and I talk Christian stuff. He told me
that if you observe your thoughts you'll find that one thought
follows another thought, as you might expect, but if you look
a little closer you'll see there's a gap between the thoughts.
A lot of Buddhists believe that gap is their true home. They
suggest we try to gently expand those gaps. Because if there's
one thing filling those gaps, it's lovingness.

*

A friend of mine had been dry for a long time then a couple
of crises blew up and he ended up drinking a bit and taking a
few drugs. He got himself clean again, but drug dealers kept

contacting him, trying to sell him stuff. I said, dob them in. He wouldn't do that. But I would. So many of the people I've met and worked with, who've been in the same situation as my friend, have had to drop all their friends and get away, because their friends want to drag them back into drink and drugs. You are the company you keep. If you watch people, you'll see they change depending on the company they're in.

If you want to stay clean you need to find new company or look for those in your environment who can help you. I became a different person because of the old gals at Ashfield. They became my aunts, and they were good company.

I've kept diverse and different company in my journey through life, for good and for bad. My inner circle now seems to bring out the best version of me: whether it's the Dalai Lama in Dharamsala or Ilya in Bangkok, they encourage and allow me to be the most fulfilled and complete version of me. Their generous and loving support is helping me cross the chasms I allowed to open up between me and my children.

The Sunday congregation at Ashfield gives me a lot too. It's been building up the last year or so, so I know I'm on the right track when I talk about personal development and growing, turning yourself around. I hope to give to them as much as they lovingly give me.

*

When my father died it was terrible. I'd just been named an Australian National Treasure and I was on my way to the celebratory dinner when Dad rang. He said, I've got to go to hospital because I've got fluid in my lungs. The tests the hospital ran revealed that there was more: he had cancer of the liver.

If I had to describe Dad's death, it would be scratch marks all the way down the wall. He didn't want to go. He didn't go gently, just as Dylan Thomas recommended we shouldn't. He raged against his dying light. It took some years and it was very difficult, especially for Mum. I remember her telling me that Dad was really suffering in hospital, and she'd said to him it's all right to go. He told her to shut up.

It wasn't nice, death never is, but Dad's death wasn't a nice time at all. I used to visit him in hospital, and after a while he just closed down. All softness and kindness seemed to leave him. He was filled with petty hatred for the nurses and other carers. I think the cancer had got to his brain. Mum tried hard to be a comfort to him. She wanted to be with him when he died, but of course it was on one of those brief occasions when she stepped out of the room that his life ended. It was brutal. It took me a long time to cry for Dad, and that only happened when I was able to step back and see the tremendous achievements of his life. The more I've been able to see him as a human being, instead of simply a force in my life, the more I can admire him and love him.

Mum died about five years after Dad. Her dying was very different.

Mum never wanted to be a nuisance, so she said to me, you don't have to come so often, Bill, but I did, and we got close towards the end. For that I'm thankful.

One of the things I learned from my relationship with my parents is that when your needs aren't fulfilled as a child, you look for a sense of belonging, of feeling loved and feeling complete, forever after. You search for everything that would normally have been supplied by one or two people, your parents, from everyone you meet. And if you don't get it, you'll always be on the lookout for it. I think I've been searching most of my life for more understanding of me, more acceptance of who I am. I've ended up looking for it in everybody, and have probably only recently started to find it, and to find myself.

CHAPTER TWELVE

THE HOLIEST OF
THE HOMELESS

I remember hearing the story of the Dalai Lama's escape from
Tibet in 1959, when I was a teenager – it piqued my interest
in this intriguing man and his occupied country. And when I
was a young child I was interested in the Chinese Communist
Party's victory in China in 1949. But I didn't know much
about Tibet and the Dalai Lama until I purchased His
Holiness's book *My Land and My People* in 1962. I devoured
every page.

I think it's fair to say that my life has been a spiritual quest.
Why did this book appeal to me as a teenager when my peers
were reading Jack Kerouac and Ian Fleming? Why was I more
fascinated with the film *The Ten Commandments* than *Around*

the World in 80 Days? This searching had obviously begun long before I found the Wayside and underwent that profound experience of the Voice that resulted in me leaving my job as a research engineer and working full-time at the Chapel.

At the Chapel I encountered people of all religions, and also of none, and I soon ended up running a monthly Spiritual Forum where we invited people from all faiths to talk and share their beliefs and doubts with us and each other. There I heard the stories of Christians, Muslims, Jews, Buddhists, Hindus, Sikhs and followers of the Children of God, the Hari Krishnas, the Bhagwan – you name it, they were all there. It was a very exciting time for me, hearing first-hand from those who really had something profoundly spiritual to say.

But in my wildest dreams I never imagined that my spiritual journey would take me to Dharamsala, in India, where the exiled Tibetan community settled after fleeing Tibet, the place that the Dalai Lama now calls 'home'. Reading the Dalai Lama's autobiography as an impressionable, questing teenager, I never thought that decades later I would not only meet the author, but that he would think of us as friends. You might as well have told the young me that I was destined to meet James Bond in the Bahamas or be sent by George Smiley to sleuth behind the Iron Curtain.

*

At the Wayside Chapel, I met several Tibetan Buddhists, but it wasn't until I came to Ashfield in 1986 that my involvement with the Tibetan people developed and deepened. Very early in my time at Ashfield, I went to a Tibetan celebration on the North Shore of Sydney and discovered that the Tibetan community was in need of a site to teach Tibetan dancing and customs to their young people.

I invited them to use our church hall in Ashfield. So on Saturday afternoons young Tibetans dressed in their silken Buddhist finery would learn about the lives and practices of their people and their lost homeland, while our Tongan choir, dressed in their traditional grass skirts, practised Christian hymns in the church.

What I didn't realise was that both Tibetans and Tongans love cricket! In summer, during the intervals between both of their practices, the Tongans and Tibetans would squeeze into the Tongans' chrome-plated jalopies to listen to Test matches between Australia and India. Grass shawls and silken robes rubbed shoulders together in the cars.

After a few months my congregation asked if a representative of the Tibetan people could speak at one of our services, so I invited Gyalsay Tulku Rinpoche to join the congregation one Sunday morning. He turned up dressed in his Tibetan Lama finery and was warmly welcomed by the congregation.

Gyalsay spoke movingly about his life and the Tibetan struggle. He told the congregation that when the Chinese Communist Party invaded Tibet they captured his brother and slowly killed him. They cut a little bit of his skin off each day until he was dead. Gyalsay had escaped with the Dalai Lama across the mountains to India.

After that service, Gyalsay and I became firm friends. We had a lot in common. He and I were both missioning in a big city, and although our religions might be different, the problems we faced were the same. We often talked about kids in trouble. Gyalsay used to spend time 'incognito' helping children in need. He often invited me to special Buddhist events. From him I learned how to chant and meditate. In 1992 Gyalsay invited me to a special dinner at Parliament House to welcome the Dalai Lama to Australia. He introduced me to him and told him of the work I did.

Some time later I received a terrible phone call. Gyalsay had died of a massive heart attack. His followers were shocked and distraught. I remember going down to his centre in Balmain, in Sydney's inner west, and finding many of them confused as to how to behave. While devastated that he had died, they were also excited at the thought of his impending rebirth. I agreed to support the group while they went through their mourning process until a new leader was found for the centre. I missed Gyalsay a lot.

On the occasion of the Dalai Lama's next visit to Sydney, in 1996, I was invited to welcome him on stage to give his public lecture at the Sydney Entertainment Centre. I wrote the speech of my life, even quoting Robert Kennedy, who said that people who stand up for others against injustice send 'forth a tiny ripple of hope, and crossing each other from a million different centers of energy and daring, those ripples build a current that can sweep down the mightiest wall of oppression and resistance'. I said that I truly believed that Jesus and His Holiness could not but be friends, and that His Holiness was the epitome of a good Christian and a living embodiment of the most holy loving kindness. I was very nervous, as not only was the Entertainment Centre filled with thousands of people but proceedings were being relayed to thousands more in the park outside. His Holiness seemed moved by what I said and gave me a white silk scarf when the function ended.

The Entertainment Centre emptied and I wandered around the area which had a few moments before been filled with people, in a bit of a daze after all that had happened. The next thing I knew, His Holiness was back in the centre looking for me. He hugged me and told me what a good job I was doing. I will treasure that moment for the rest of my life.

That event created an even closer tie between me and the Tibetan community. I was invited to speak at many functions marking His Holiness's birthdays and other major events in the lives of Tibetan people.

A year later I was lined up at the entrance to the Wentworth Hotel to welcome His Holiness back to Australia. A very old and frail Tibetan Buddhist monk was standing opposite me. As His Holiness entered, this old man fell to his knees and kissed the Dalai Lama's feet. It was such a tender loving action it brought tears to my eyes. It reminded me what true humility is about. My welcome paled in comparison.

After his press conference His Holiness opened his arms to me and drew me into a hug, then presented me with another special white silk scarf, wrapping it around my neck. I wrapped the scarf around him as well, so the scarf contained both of us. He told me he thought I was a good Buddhist. And I said he was a good Christian. 'But I'm not a Christian, Bill,' he would tell me later. 'Neither was Jesus,' I retorted.

We both laughed as the press went mad with photos. I took the opportunity to ask His Holiness if I could interview him for television and he graciously agreed. I was beginning to realise that we were developing a special rapport.

At the appointed time the next day His Holiness swept into the interview room followed by an almost endless line of disciples. I really wanted to explore the way the old monk had fallen to his knees and kissed His Holiness's feet, and I asked him the question 'Who are you?'

'I'm a simple monk,' he replied.

'No,' I boldly responded, 'you're more than that. Many of your followers would die for you. I'd probably die for you too. I can't think of anyone who would die for the Pope! Who *are* you?'

I have pondered his answer ever since. 'I am the teaching,' he said. At that moment I looked right into his eyes and somehow saw right through them to the Buddhist Dharma. At the same time, in my head, I found myself looking into Jesus's eyes and saw through *those* eyes into the indescribable peace and majesty of God. 'I am the teaching.' Right there and then I found those great 'I am' statements of Jesus, like 'I am the way, the truth and the life', making real sense to me.

On His Holiness's next visit to Australia I was invited to host an interfaith service in Parliament House, Canberra. I was also invited to a luncheon in Melbourne and on the next day shared with the Dalai Lama in the filming of the TV show *MasterChef*. It was the first time I had spent a significant amount of time with him and followed him from function to function. I noticed that the way he coped was by simply being himself. For most people that is very hard to do because we change to adapt to the company we're keeping. I noticed that His Holiness didn't do that at all and felt it was probably what kept him sane in the madness that is a Dalai

Lama tour, when he can barely go to the bathroom without being followed by an entourage.

With the Dalai Lama what you see is what you get. No airs and graces; just a man in a robe with leather boots and a tennis visor to shade his eyes from the bright lights. His powerful intellect is sometimes hidden in the noise of the event. But it's only somebody with a powerful intellect who can be themselves and answer truthfully from within themselves in the immediacy of the intense questioning, the sycophancy, the political posturing and one-upmanship of a Dalai Lama event. It is only a truly humble person who does not become blinded by the fawning crowd and start to believe his own press.

At one event His Holiness spoke of how he had been talking about the merits of democracy for a long time and how he felt he'd better put his actions where his words were. Subsequently, in 2011, he gave up his political power as unelected leader of the Tibetans so his people could choose a parliament and a prime minister. I cannot think of one other leader who has voluntarily given up power in this way.

*

I'm often asked how I got the Dalai Lama out to Ashfield. The simple answer is that I invited him. I said, come out and

Here I am with His Holiness the Dalai Lama (above) and Dwayne, one of our regulars at Exodus (below).

feed the hungry, and he did. It was a battle, though, to keep the toffs away. I stood firm and the event was just for the poor and needy, the people who really need fertile soil.

Everyone loved him. There were a lot of homeless kids there, and His Holiness became a doting grandfather, telling them to be good boys and girls, to go to school and study. He helped serve food to 400 people that day, and blessed them all. Dwayne, one of our regular homeless guys, didn't wash his hand for a month, but then he didn't wash anyway! Later we went into the church and His Holiness placed his white scarf around the cross. We've never taken it away.

Apparently, the Dalai Lama talks about that visit a lot, being here and serving meals, because it was the first time he'd been invited to do something like that. Perhaps I did it because I just see him as a human being, making the best of his life in the face of his people's oppression. No amount of frenzied obsequiousness from his Western followers can make up for that, and I think that in the midst of his determination to spread a message of love and compassion he may well feel lonely and long for his true home.

I think recognising loneliness in someone else – me – was a relief for His Holiness. It's nice to sit with someone who's in the same spot, although of course his loneliness may be just a projection on my part. But there must be loneliness in being placed on a pedestal and stood back from and that's what people tend to do around him. That might be why we get on. I cross the artificial divide placed around him and treat him as I would anyone else I admire and respect.

*

In 2017 I stepped down off a very small plane onto the tarmac at Kangra Airport in the state of Himachal Pradesh in northern India. There to greet me was a young woman, Kando, with a driver and a car. Kando had been newly seconded to the Dalai Lama's 'Department of Bringing in Distinguished Guests', she told me, and I didn't want to disappoint her by telling her that I was simply Bill from Sydney.

I had a day before I was to have my audience with His Holiness, so Kando put me in the car and showed me around.

We visited the Tibetan Museum, where there's a wall covered in 147 photos of those monks who have self-immolated in protest over the Chinese occupation of Tibet. I was struck by the kindness and compassion in their faces, and wondered at the bravery needed to embrace such a painful death. We also travelled to a 'children's village', an orphanage by any other name. Many Tibetan parents living under Chinese rule in Tibet walk across the Himalayas with their newborns and leave their babies in Dharamsala, so that the children will have a proper Tibetan upbringing. There are dormitories of cots for the babies, then childcare and then school. Kando herself had graduated from a children's village. She went on to university, taking a master's degree in international relations. I idly asked her how old she was before she saw her parents again after they'd left her at the children's village. She answered, 'Last year, when I was twenty-nine.' She hadn't seen her mother and father for twenty-nine years! In the humblest and most compassionate way she told me that they were toothless, illiterate peasants. What a sacrifice they'd made to ensure their daughter's future! What love they'd shown.

I was really touched when Khando said to me, 'When I get married, will you come and give me away?'

'Of course!' I replied.

*

Then it was time to go and see His Holiness. It was an absolutely beautiful morning but nothing was brighter than the smile he gave me when he greeted me. We hugged tightly as he called me 'my dear friend from Australia' and reminisced about his visit to Ashfield and the effect it had on him. We agreed that it is how we treat the poorest of the poor and those in most need that defines us as human beings.

His Holiness talked about compassion and lovingness, one human being to another, which led me to tell him the story of the Korean Comfort Woman statue at our church. I told him how Korean people make pilgrimage from all over the world to visit that statue, to stand there and cry, to remember and do homage. Just a week earlier a group of Korean parents whose children had drowned when a ferry capsized had visited the statue. One father and mother, whose daughter had drowned while on the phone to them, had told me that my church, where homeless people look after the Korean Comfort Woman statue and where they had seen homeless people eating, had made their hearts feel warm for the first time in ages.

I found myself looking into His Holiness's eyes as our conversation became increasingly intimate and personal and felt I got a glimpse of his desire to use his teachings to relate at a human as well as a spiritual level.

He talked about the power of love, saying that lovingness is at the core of all that is, and that the Chinese government, which continues to oppress his people, needed to act with compassion, tolerance and discipline. Nevertheless, 'We need to be grateful to those people we are in conflict with,' he said, 'because they teach us so much about ourselves. Once you truly understand that, you can feel sorry for those people who do not have those sorts of feelings.' I was reminded of the prayer I'd got from a bishop in Africa who prayed for the very people who'd raped and murdered his daughter. The bishop and the Dalai Lama were on the same page, understanding that forgiveness and love are at the heart of all human beings and are the only way we can truly live and grow.

I took off my glasses and perhaps rather boldly asked the Dalai Lama to take his off too. I asked him to look me directly in the eyes. For a moment we both vanished and went somewhere timeless and then came back with a jolt. Only, we were different when we came back – that's what I felt, at any rate. To me it was what Jesus meant when he talked about finding yourself; you have to lose yourself first.

The Dalai Lama was deeply affected too, and hugged me, explaining that when we like someone our pupils dilate. We lose ourselves in the other person, in humanity, in love and compassion.

His Holiness asked an aide to fetch something for Him. The aide returned with a crystal obelisk mounted on a wooden base. With a black marker the Dalai Lama drew a cross on the crystal. 'This is for you,' he said, 'from the Holy Spirit.' As we parted he hugged me tightly and with tears in his eyes said, 'I'm so glad you came to see me, my old friend. So glad.' I hope his happiness was the equal of mine.

*

The homeless live cheek by jowl with the wealthy throughout the world, just like the Dalai Lama and China, rubbing up alongside each other on either side of the Himalayas.

In the 1970s, when Frank Theeman was hellbent on redeveloping the Kings Cross area and Victoria Street, there were two things I saw that I'll never forget, both in Woolloomooloo. The first was when I was walking at night and came across a group of homeless people who'd built a bonfire in an old, demolished square. They were sitting around the fire in the warmth, and that was all they had. The second was coming across a series of old terrace houses slated for demolition with gaping holes in the floors, so that you had to walk carefully or you'd fall from one storey to another. Between the dangerous holes were bundles of blankets, and in the blankets I found homeless kids.

Why are so many in the world homeless? For many, it's because of the way wealth is distributed. One reason, in Australia, might be that human beings are very proud creatures and the last thing they want is for family to know they're down on their luck. At Exodus and the Bill Crews Charitable Trust we offer help with no strings attached: no moralising, no reporting to parents or guardians, just food and shelter and a willingness to sit and listen, allowing the homeless person their dignity.

One homeless man dropped dead at our food van. An ambulance came and tried to revive him, but couldn't. Who was he? One of the volunteers said he'd been coming to the van a long time, but they only knew him as Fred. There was nothing in his pockets and all he had with him was his bag of clothes – no ID, no clues. I was upset and disappointed that although Fred had been coming to the van for years, no one knew his story.

I went on the radio and appealed for help in establishing Fred's identity. Women rang in from all over Australia, thinking he might have been their dad, an uncle, a long-lost brother. This went on for months until finally the police found a thumbprint from before 1980 when Fred had been arrested for vagrancy, and we had a name, but not much else.

Rumour had it that Fred came from Ireland, so I went on Irish radio and, just as in Australia, letters rolled in from everywhere in Ireland, hundreds of them, but none of the leads went anywhere.

And then, somehow, the police found Fred's great-niece in Leeds, England, so when I next travelled to the UK I took his ashes over with me. I met the great-niece and her family, and she told me that Fred had simply left home one day; that his mum wrote to him every day but never got a reply. The family thought that he may have followed a romance that didn't work out. His mother and father died not knowing what had become of their son. The great-niece promised to take Fred's ashes to Ireland to inter with his parents' graves.

It took nearly a year to find out who Fred was. I remember wondering at the time if anyone could really vanish off the face of the earth and not have anybody miss them. I'm glad that in this case I was proved wrong, and we found those who'd missed Fred for so long. It reaffirmed to me what Jesus said about knowing every feather on the bird: everyone matters, somehow everyone matters.

Some of the homeless people who find their way to Ashfield have nothing but their bearing. And really that's all any of us have in this life: whatever you build up can be torn away in five minutes, even less, as so many Australians discovered in the devasting bushfires of 2019–20. When all else is gone, all we have left is our integrity.

RULE #12

**The healthier you get, the healthier your relationships
with those around you will be. This is where
determination kicks in as you will get blowback
from people who don't want change and are being
forced to form new relationships with you.**

As we grow emotionally and spiritually, we experience
'growing pains' when those around us may not be on their
own journey of growth.

I wasn't able to reconcile my relationship with my father
until after he died; not until recently did I begin to feel some
compassion for him. It took time and experience, and it
was only really when I walked the streets of Walthamstow
in north-east London, where, as a little boy, my dad had
picked up horse manure to sell, that my heart opened to him.
I walked the streets Dad and his brother walked. I walked
past the school he went to as a tiny boy and the park where
his own father cut his throat when Dad was but six years old.
I could see the pain and the suffering, the hurt and the loss. It
took a long time. But finally I could begin to understand Dad.

When one person in a relationship embarks on some personal growth, the other sometimes gets left behind in the old paradigm of what they had together. Should you hold yourself back, essentially betray yourself, for fear of the distance you might create between you and someone you love? My answer is a resounding no. Your changing offers the other person a chance to change too.

You can't actually stunt another person's growth, but people try. It's sad, because the person trying can't move forward and grow themselves. And meanwhile they're retarding someone else's progress. It's criminal to do that. Even if you think what someone else is doing is mad, foolish, crazy – like giving up engineering to work for a pittance with the poor.

If you truly love someone, you'll sit beside them in their journey; you won't try to stop them. It's only in the letting go that they'll eventually come back in some form. If you try to hold on to them, they'll end up hating you.

Your growing offers someone else the chance to grow, and if they don't want to take it, that's their decision. Sometimes they can't see it, or fear stops them from wanting to grow. I've seen with my kids that what's happening to me, as I embrace new 'families' and communities around the world and throw myself into 'belonging', is offering them something I couldn't offer them before when I was emotionally paralysed. I'm working hard to fix that now.

I've noticed that the more I discover myself, the more I can give myself away and sit beside someone, but you can't sit beside someone until you've got something in yourself that you can give away, something that you know you are. The more you discover yourself the more you realise you can't change other people, but you can sit beside them while they change themselves. I think back to my old orator mate Webster; he was someone who offered others the chance to grow. There was no holding on to anyone; he just offered the opportunity to think and reflect.

Recently I found myself channelling my father. Someone I loved was struggling with an issue and I found my father's words coming from my mouth. At first I was horrified, then I spoke about it with my psychotherapist, Dr Wotton.

'Didn't your father ever do any loving things or say anything loving?' Dr Wotton asked.

'Of course he did,' I answered.

'Well, that's what's happening. That's the loving side of your father you can now accept and embrace.'

It was like opening a floodgate of repressed memories. Memories of all the loving things that my father had done for me. As I progress I discover more and more the loving parts of my father – they are in me. There was a huge loving side to Dad and I had spent years actively denying it. In the past that search for a loving father got me into heaps of trouble.

Particularly with authority figures like the Church. It really damaged my intimate relationships too.

The father figure I was searching for I now find and accept within myself. I can now both build and father the loving community I have always yearned to be part of. I can now move forward personally too. My father was always critical of my friendships and relationships. Consequently, I kept them hidden or felt guilty about them. All that has now fallen away and I can embrace my intimate relationships unreservedly.

What I have discovered is that nothing and no one can fill the gaps in our being. We can only do that ourselves. Relationships can help us come to terms with our own holes but only we can fix them. Of course the love of others can help us heal ourselves. But it's not a Band-Aid to cover a gaping hole; it is a means of finding healing within. It's the love for me from within me that heals me and it's the unconditional love I give to others that allows me to love myself and heal.

I feel as if my very DNA has been rearranged. It's a true coming in from the cold, and it's nice and it's cuddly and lovely. Here I am, seventy-five years old, and I feel my life is just beginning! It's never too late for the winds of change to blow.

BACK TO THE JUNGLE

Calais, even on a summer's day, can feel grey and unforgiving. Like its mirror-image, Dover, on the other side of La Manche, just fifty kilometres away, it is a ferry port, a border city, an entry and exit point, a place where the population ebbs and flows with those coming in and out like the tide. On a clear day, you can see the white cliffs across the Channel. From inside the Calais Jungle, such optimistic horizons – with their promise of hope – are not visible.

Everything in life comes full circle and I find myself back at the place I started this story, in the Calais Jungle, among the last, the least and the lost of this world, which is how I felt that day at the Narcotics Anonymous meeting. 'I'm

Bill from Australia,' I said in English. 'English! English!' some exclaimed, maybe hoping that I could help them get to England. 'No, I'm from Australia,' I told them. And just poured out my story. Those kind people whom I didn't know listened.

'I'm Bill from Australia,' I began. 'I've had two stuffed marriages and relationships that have all gone to hell. My children have suffered from that and are still suffering.' I emptied out my heart, canvassing just about my entire life. Everyone listened carefully as what I said was translated into French. And all this happened not in a solid building, not with counsellors present, not among 'respectable' middle-class people, but with the world's rejects. Not only were these people refugees that the world did not want, they were drug-affected Muslim refugees, which placed them on a lower level still. Right then I felt at one with their pain, and couldn't see any way that they could possibly help me. It felt like the end, and it could not have come in a more appropriate location. I was in a tent on a snow-covered flood plain in Europe, a long way from home, with a group of rejected, ignored, abandoned refugees.

Yet as I spoke my truth, all my lonely years of feeling put down and rejected fell away. The refugees listened until I was out of words and then they came forward with open arms and welcomed me in. I finally came home. I was among those who had nothing, but they gave me everything and more than I could ever imagine.

There was no choir, no priest, no religion, just acceptance and love. They gave me my life back. They didn't judge me because I hadn't experienced their addiction, they just accepted me. 'Welcome, Bill,' they said and hugged me.

From that point on, I decided to live my life differently. I think I have. I hope I have. It hasn't been as difficult as I thought it would be; it hasn't been nearly as difficult as the lives of my comforters in the Jungle. Two moments have been pivotal in my life so far: one was that day walking up the stairs to the café at the Wayside Chapel, forty years ago, and the second was my unconditional acceptance by loving strangers in the Jungle. Somehow, at that very moment, I came in from the cold.

I'll never forget those people in Calais: they gave me my life back and I decided I had to somehow outwardly acknowledge that because of them my life had changed. I wondered what I could do to mark their generosity and my 'rebirth' and decided to throw out all my clothing and only wear black in honour of those brave, compassionate people. From that day on I've honoured that decision and I now only wear black to show in a physical way how I've changed.

*

I was in Calais again last year. Even though the French authorities had dismantled the Jungle, a lot of people had moved back there, and it had started to build up again.

To get into the camp I had to get past maybe a dozen busloads of police in full riot gear on both sides of the road. I was with Clare Moseley of Care4Calais and they wouldn't let us in without a pass, even though she runs the charity that does most to help the desperate who flock to the new Jungle. We went back to Clare's place and she got on the internet, googled 'Official Pass', and printed out a couple, handed them to the authorities and they let us in. This is the madness of it.

Clare also took me to Dunkirk, forty kilometres along the coast, where the police had destroyed another refugee camp and left people to die in the snow. The mayors of those coastal towns look on the refugees as cockroaches. We drove off the highway into a forest where all the leaves had fallen and snow was thick on the ground.

Within minutes, hundreds of people emerged from the trees, mainly young Iraqi and Kurdish males, all skinny, malnourished and bitterly cold. The police had smashed their phones and ripped their tents, making it almost impossible for them to survive. Our convoy brought food, clothes, sleeping bags, chargers for phones and phone batteries. There were only five of us, including Clare, but the refugees formed a queue so we could give them what they needed.

My job was to monitor the queue and direct each refugee in turn to the vans handing out food and clothing. I decided to look each one of them in the eye, hug them and say 'Welcome'. Many of them thanked me and one said, 'It's lovely to have someone say that, just lovely. I haven't been hugged for years.' I'd ask them how long they'd been away from home, struggling to survive, and they'd say things like five years; my family's getting really worried because they're running out of money and they can't send me much more. When I asked why they had left their homeland, a look of terror would come over them and they'd whisper 'Daesh'. They were all fleeing the horrors of Islamic extremism.

There were doctors, lawyers, specialists – people who could add to a country. Looking into their eyes all I could see was our common humanity, but these poor people had to head back into the snow and God knows what else and maybe freeze to death far from their homes and loved ones. They'd run for freedom, only to find that 'freedom' locked the gates so they couldn't get in. England, Australia and other nations which view themselves as bastions of freedom and democracy just tell them to bugger off and hope they'll die quietly somewhere out of sight. So I just kept hugging each and every one of them, because that's what I'd had done for me when I found myself lost and without hope in Calais. I'll continue to go back to help feed, clothe and hug whoever I can.

*

In all the interviews I do, I'm always asked what the personal cost to me is of my work. I guess it's because I have this enormous library of stories that are dark and are difficult terrain for any human being to hold on to, be a part of and be involved in: Calais, tainted blood, the comfort women and caring for the homeless and needy during the coronavirus pandemic. I understand why I'm asked that, because it's a compelling question that others want to know the answer to. Where do I draw my nourishment from when I'm on the frontline? All I can say is I draw my strength from whatever is behind that Voice that spoke to me. It said don't worry; it said it'll be all right, everything might seem terrible at times, but it'll be okay as well. There was a power behind that Voice which is not of this world, as Jesus says. When I get really down I'm nourished by the power behind the Voice, whatever it is, because I couldn't do my work on my own, I really couldn't.

When I go to places like Calais or when I'm among needy homeless people in the midst of a pandemic, I'm saying to that Voice: I'm doing what you told me to do. I might die, but you will nourish me anyway. I'm not doing my work to get to heaven, whatever that is, or for earthly reward or recognition. It's about doing the right thing. What's really important is loving compassion. Be loving, be compassionate, be steadfast. Be true. That's what the Voice told me to do.

I'm doing my best. The thing from my end is that I can say I'm doing my best.